The Curated Experience:

Engineering Customer Service to Build Loyalty

AMAS TENUMAH

ISBN:
ISBN-13:

DEDICATION

In memory of my mother, Christie, I miss you every day. I never got a chance to say thank you for raising us. I think you would be proud to see the young adults Aly and Laye have grown up to be. Thank you for everything, I love you.

In memory of my father, William. You were my hero! I miss you terribly.

In memory of my brother, Bobby. I see your face every time I see your nephew. I miss you.

vos oblivione delebitur

Foreword

"The customers is *always* right!" The creation of this phrase is one of the greatest mistakes ever made. Nothing could be further from the truth and I blame this phrase as one of the sources of contention between customers and the corporations that serve them today.

Anyone who has actually worked with customers, knows that customers aren't always right. In fact, customers are often wrong. Customers break things, forget steps, misunderstand instruction , and are probably the root cause of many of their own problems. Now, before you throw this book away in disgust for the suggestion of such heresy , wait just one minute. Yes, customers are *not* always right. However, wrong customers are *still* customers. As such, whether right or wrong, creating a curated customer experience is critical for creating successful organizations. No, our customers are *not* perfect. In fact, no one is. However, despite our imperfections, we can still create amazing experiences that cultivate positive relationships. These positive relationships are proven to create customer loyalty and long-term success.

Amas Tenumah's *The Curated Experience*, shows organizations that decisions that are "good for business", yet come at the cost of the customer experience, have a drastic negative impact on the future success of the organization. As a master at operationalizing customer experience, Amas shows how to turn service theories into practical applications that deliver positive bottom-line results. Whether it's the application of customer feedback programs or developing customer success frameworks, when you spend just a few minutes with Amas, it's clear that he's truly devoted to his customers and his teams exemplify a truly customer-centric culture.

Unfortunately, too many organizations have given up trying to delight their customers and business decisions are often made behind closed doors, by individuals who have never or may never actually speak with a customer. One-sided customer-impacting decisions, while done in the name of "good business", often lead to tragic consequences that derail even the most ingenious product inventions or the soundest market strategy.

Luckily, we have battle-tested experience process experts, such as Amas, who have proven their experience acumen that can guide us as we become liberated from the traditional structures of business-centric, customer fickle strategies that erase any potential of customer loyalty. Amas shows the way for any organization to create truly personalized, continuous, and contextual customer-centric experiences.

Regardless of the size or industry, Amas shows how we should develop customer journey maps, where to focus our efforts in mining service data, and how to create effective customer feedback channels for service improvement. Wisdom says, "if you can't measure it, you can't manage it" and we live in the world of big data. With numberless options and permutations of information available at our fingertips, it's critical that organizations clearly define the right data points that will guide them towards developing positive customer experiences. Amas cuts through the world of fuzzy service metrics and gets to the core of what truly matters to customers.

If you're starting out in a new venture, or want to turn around a struggling service organization, *The Curated Experience* is your manual to setting up the right structure and framework for positive customer experience strategy. Amas will show you how to empower your service teams, and create a customer-centric experience culture that will create the foundation for future success in your organization. You can then turn your attentions to recruiting other service experts to join in your cause. With your empowering processes in place, and the right people aligned around the mission of serving customers, you'll be ready to go out and deliver the type of experiences that your customers expect and deserve. And you'll keep them coming back for more.

Staying ahead of the competition when the bar is set so low is easy. But winning the hearts and minds of your customers, and creating loyal customers takes experience, strategy, smart data, and hard work. If you're ready for change, *The Curated Experience*, is the first step forward. The practical advice, and sound strategy you'll find in it will ensure that you will create the right foundation for the system you need to connect with your customers and deliver the right results. Following Amas' strategy you'll see exactly how to utilize the powerful tools available to experienced professionals and ensure that research, insight, and data are all weaved into improving the customer experience so that it delivers the business results you want most.

The power of the customer is ever more present in today's digitally-connected social world. With the upload of a picture, a 140-character tweet, or a post to a close group of friends the reputation and future of a business hangs in the balance. Too much is at stake to leave it to chance. The choice isn't between customers or profit, both must co-exist. The business management wizard Peter Drucker set the record straight when he said, "the purpose of a business is to create [and keep] a customer." Too many organizations place their top priorities in the finance, sales, production, management, and legal aspects of their business. However, it's experience that leads to the attraction of new customers and the retention of existing customers. The curated and cultivated experience is the path to winning customers and creating positive business results.

Biography

Flavio Martins is the vice president of operations and customer service at DigiCert, Inc. and the author of *Win the Customer: 70 Simple Rules for Sensational Service*. His customer service team is consistently recognized by industry analysts for it best-in-class customer support and experience differentiation. Huffington Post has named Flavio as one of the most influential social customer service professionals, and by ICMI as one of the most influential people in customer service. In addition to overseeing day-to-day operations, marketing, and customer support, Flavio runs his award-winning blog: http://winthecustomer.com.

Amas Tenumah

Contents

Introduction

The Empowered Customer

We are in the age of the empowered consumer. The all-powerful consumer is in the driver's seat. The consumer has unlimited information literally at their fingertips anytime, anywhere – and at little or no cost to them. The almighty consumer knows all. There are even corporate Edward Snowden-style leaks about the inner workings of your company to further inform the customer. On top of that, the barrier of switching providers is so low that the empowered consumer will ditch your service at the slightest inkling of a bad experience. Not only will they defect, they also have a huge megaphone to broadcast your dirty laundry to the world and bring you to your knees. For self-preservation's sake, every organization is supposed to be so scared that they will be forced to treat customers better. There should be ongoing one-upmanship in the customer experience world, with everyone trying to out-experience the other, all to avoid mass exodus of the all empowered consumer.

I don't know about you, but as a consumer, I don't feel empowered. I still go online to shop on websites that I find confusing. I swipe my own credit card, bag my own groceries, and pump my own gas while paying more for all of it. Do I have enough information about products and services? Yes, a dizzying amount of information. So much information that I am confused and paralyzed. Do I have more choices? Well yes, so many choices that it takes me 30 minutes to decide on a box of cereal! Is the barrier of switching lower? Sure, I have fantasized about ditching my insurance company for another because of my experiences with them - they didn't seem to get the memo that I am empowered. The problem, from what I can figure anyway, is that the competition isn't any better. In fact, it appears that they all got together and decided to take allegiances to aim for mediocrity across the board. So yes, the barrier of switching is fairly low in many cases, but with such a low bar if I switched providers, I would be trading one flavor of crap for another. I am so empowered that I can't call customer service in front of my young son because there is more than a 50 percent chance that I might yell obscenities into the poorly designed IVRs. There are probably more bad IVRs today than there were ten years ago. When organizations intentionally or unintentionally end up understaffed, they don't move heaven and earth to fix it and they don't overspend to make it right. The customer bares the brunt of it. Not only is there scant data showing a vast improvement in customer service due to consumer empowerment, There is not a long line of people telling me how much the customer experience has improved.

Clearly, great customer experiences have not become the norm. The truth is, the threat that was supposed to motivate organizations to improve experiences never really materialized for a couple of reasons. For one thing, the so-called megaphone turned out to be the exception and not the rule. Sure you can cite examples from Netflix and BOA involving customers being able to drive change, but they continue to be the exception, not the rule. Are organizations generally afraid of social media backlash? Of course. Have they hired more interns to man Twitter and Facebook? Yes. Has it raised the bar of customer-centricity? I would say, no.

The second thing is that all of the empowering information that we have at our fingertips isn't making consumers empowered, or more informed about their buying decisions. Not only is it actually making things more confusing and time-consuming, the source of a lot of our information is by searching online, and it is increasingly biased. In an effort to personalize our experience, our search results are no longer objective.

I continue to be optimistic, the irony is that in the age of the empowered and demanding consumer, there is actually more opportunity to delight customers. Instead of playing defense and worrying about what the customer mob might pressure you into doing, there are proactive steps to take. The fact is that customer experience will always be a point of differentiation, and it might actually be easier to deliver an exceptional experience today than ever before. With the sheer amount of data available, the days of guessing why your customer might be contacting you is almost over and you can now very safely anticipate your customer's needs and deliver. If you still need to be motivated by fear to deliver great customer experiences, here is a little additional fear for you, though you probably won't suffer the same fate that United Airlines did in the guitar video, your customers will simply defect to your competitor without much fanfare.

Personalized, Continuous, and Contextual

I have spent the last eight years telling anyone who would listen that the customer experience is the most important thing in business today, and I believe it. Is it a biased opinion? Absolutely!

I do want to take things a step further. Delivering a great customer experience for your customers should be your primary objective - growths and profits should be a byproduct of delighting customers. I have spent my entire career on a customer facing team. It is common knowledge that customers want or may even need a personalized experience that is not only continuous but always contextual. The way to deliver this is to intentionally hand craft every customer experience and to focus on the three underlying elements of every interaction - liberating structures, empowered people, and data driven technology.

We are smarter today about building structures that liberate instead of inhibit. There is a generation of customer experience professionals that are dynamite when empowered. The explosions of data driven technological capabilities mean that we can provide a service experience today that can meet, or in many cases exceed customers' expectations without breaking the bank.

I have had the pleasure of working with thousands of customer experience professionals with varying levels of responsibilities within the customer service arena over the last 15 years or so. The overwhelming majority are service oriented, many got into the customer experience profession by chance but choose to stay because they believe they can make a difference. They face obstacles daily, many outside their control but they press on. They continue to be the biggest well of ideas to improve the customer experience.

I wrote this book for leaders in the customer experience field, particularly those who have responsibility for leading teams that have direct contact with customers. These leaders run customer interaction centers of all sizes and come to work every day to make a difference in the lives of their employees and customers. I want to explore these three ingredients in greater detail - liberating structures, data guided technology, and empowered people. I want to share with you my experiences on how you might influence each of these ingredients. Every great customer interaction has these ingredients in varying degrees. Some interactions have data driven technology as the star of the show, while empowered people and liberating structures are behind the scenes.

The key is to be intentional about deploying these elements so that every customer interaction is without friction. Above all else, I want to start a conversation about how we can all improve customer loyalty by focusing on the customer. I want to hear about your journey as you focus on the customer experience as well, so we can learn from each other and continue curating customer experiences for the better.

If there are any topics you would like to discuss or have me elaborate on, I would love for you to reach me at amas@amastenumah.com or http://amastenumah.com

Amas Tenumah

Part One
Liberating Structure

A Hill to Die On

One spring morning, I had two very upset employees in my office. They were both in tears. One was a great frontline customer service representative and the other was her manager. I couldn't make out much of what she was saying but I heard enough to understand a customer called her an F'ing B*$%! I did my best to console them and assured them that I was on the case. Within minutes I was listening to the recordings from their interactions – there was no polishing this turd. This was a really bad call and even though my rep was a saint, the customer was relentless. Let's just say my already expansive dictionary on profanity expanded by a few more words.

Apparently, there were a half dozen similar unreported calls from this customer that were just as inflammatory sitting on our servers. I quickly reached out to my bosses, wanting a rubber-stamped approval to end our relationship with the customer. They were willing to listen and requested the customer's profile, and it turns out that he was a pretty big account. With the almighty dollar guiding our thinking, we took a left turn on Rationalization Street. We had come to the cowardly conclusion that the occasional rant and a little customer abuse was par for the course.

However, we did decide that a line needed to be drawn, and we used financial compensation to draw it. We concluded that we definitely don't pay our frontline employees enough to face these types of customers. So we established that similar calls should be immediately sent on to the supervisors and managers. Since we paid them more, they should handle them. The firing of abusive or otherwise bad customers is table stakes and simply **good business. If you do not identify and root out these customers, they will consume an inordinate amount of your resources with very little upside and will distract you from other customers..**

I asked a client a seemingly innocuous question - who is your customer? He went on for about 45 seconds and finished by saying, "practically everyone who drinks water". You shouldn't want every customer that drinks water! A foundational element in creating liberating structures during your curation journey is defining who your customer is. Maybe more importantly you should know who your customer isn't.

Once you have clarity on who your customers are, you need to find out what they want and how they want it. In simple terms, your customers are individuals and want to be treated as such. To achieve this you must create interactions that are connected and contextually relevant. Whatever your feelings are about the last sentence, consider the following statistic. Seventy percent of buying experiences are based on how the customer feels they are being treated. This means you are in the business of managing feelings. You are in the emotions business. In most cases, your success or failure has more to do with how you make your customers feel than your product or service in it of themselves. If you have responsibility for customer service or customer experience, then congratulations. I happen to think you have the most important job in your organization.

The future of your company depends a lot on how good you and your team are. Do you know who your customers are? What customers are you willing to jettison? When I say the customer experience is a hill you should be willing to die on, the definition of what "customer" means and what it doesn't mean becomes critical to building the liberating structures that guide how you treat them. This allows you to adjust your own thinking when you understand who your customer is. Get really comfortable with firing customers that do not meet the criteria for your business.

You also need to begin to see the company through your customer's eyes. Suppose you are in the business of selling wedding gowns. It would be accurate to see yourself as a clothier whose target demographic happens to be women on their wedding day. Understanding your customer, and having an outside-in view, means understanding that the business you are in is not clothing, you are in the business of helping to create one of the most important days in your customers' lives. You will view your mission in that vein, you will plan everything knowing that you are in the business of making sure that their special day goes without a hitch. No matter your goods or services, your company exists to create a great customer experience. Long term profits and growth are simply a byproduct of that mission.

Expectations

A good friend of mine shares with anyone who will listen that the reason most relationships fail is because of unmet expectations. When you have 30 seconds, watch this very short YouTube video. It's a simple trust fall exercise by two young girls that ends badly. You'll see the faller closes her eyes, fall forward, and end up flat on her face. As you and I know, the social contract of the trust fall is that you fall backwards in hopes that you'll be captured by the person standing behind you. In this video, the girl falls forward and her expectations for being caught were dashed.

Too often, your customers fall face first when they interact with you and the blame is politely put on the customer as we usually brand them as unreasonable. I drove to a store to return an unopened sheet set, confidently expecting my money back. To my chagrin, I was told that I was four days outside the window. I argued my point by pointing to the hassle-free returns sign behind the counter. In the end, I knew my goose was cooked when she uttered the three scariest words in customer service: "Our policy states …." I pressed the issue and they probably felt I had expected much more than they ever promised. I left there with the feeling that they didn't fulfill their brand promise. This chasm in expectations is at the root of customer relations issues, or any human relationship for that matter.

Trying to meet customer expectations that you haven't defined clearly is an impossible task. I think given the stakes, it is worth pausing to ask what these expectations really are. Can you articulate what your customer expects of you? Do you know who set these expectations? Did you explicitly set these expectations? Are they implicit? Are they implied because of what your competitor's practices are? In other words, is Amazon and other companies setting the expectation level for your customers?

If the goal is to close the chasm between what your customers expect of you and what you are providing, then a good place to start is being clear what these expectations are. Here are a few tips to get you started:

1. Journey Mapping – focus on the emotions and feelings through each journey map. Remember, they are not always linear (quite frankly they are seldom linear these days). In addition to feelings and emotions, capture expectations through each step and document the source of those expectations and whether you are meeting them. What you might learn is that you are making a lot of subtle promises in your marketing, on your website, and in customer service that culminate into the customer expecting far more than you are prepared to give. If you own the service recovery experience, start doing micro-journey maps. These maps focus on a very specific part of the service journey. For example you might look into the journey of customers when they attempt to make a return.

2. Mine From Your Existing Data – This is the mountain of customer feedback, calls, and emails collecting dust on your servers. They are the nuggets of customer expectations you have been in denial about. If you need inspiration, use voice/text analytics to surface experiences where your team uses those three scary words: "Our policy states…"

3. Talk to Other Companies or Their Customers -- If you are in an industry not famous for great experience, there's no need to benchmark with your peers. Instead, reach out and talk to Amazon customers. It helps you not only learn what expectations other companies you admire have set, but also helps you see where customers get these expectations from.

Closing the expectations gap certainly requires understanding and from there it can give you perspective on where to focus your attention. Now that you know where your moments of truth are, you know which of those moments have opportunities for improvement and which are downright horrible.

What if Customer Service Doesn't Matter?

There is an argument that providing great experiences is not an end, it's a means to an end. What if you could treat customers poorly and still be a profitable company? Consider this study in 2013 that looked at 200 major American brands, comparing their customer satisfaction indexes with their stock performances. It came to one sobering conclusion for someone like me who makes a living convincing anyone who will listen to care about their customers.

As it turns out, some of the most hated companies from a customer satisfaction perspective outperformed their beloved peers with much better service. Time Warner Cable, so notorious for its bad service and ranked towards the bottom of the CSAT (Customer Satisfaction), had had stock rise 450 percent over the last five years. If you are in retail and salivating at all the money you can save by firing your customer service staff, let me stop your celebration. The reason that these companies continue to thrive in the face of providing bad customer experiences has to do with the competitive landscape they operate in.

Your choices are pretty limited in certain industries, like when it comes to utilities like phone and broadband internet providers, etc. While customers want to leave, they are landlocked... for now. Frankly, these companies generally see that there is little incentive for them to improve their customer service experience. Lack of choice isn't necessarily a permanent state.. So for now, some of these companies have little incentive to improve their experience and really see no upside to doing more than to pay lip service to the customer experience.

Truth is exemption from competition, is becoming extremely rare even in historically uncompetitive industries. A while back, I got to work with a gas and electric company. Their CEO listened to me make the case for using data to improve customer experience and gave me his card. I called him expecting to hear some tactical need. I was pleasantly surprised that he wanted to talk about NPS® and whether or not it had a proven record of predicting loyalty. I told him I had seen the power of creating a system focused on removing customer friction, which in turn yields loyal customers and that it has worked like a charm for many organizations. He then I asked if I could help lay out a strategy to do the same at his company. I paused for a second so that I could set proper expectation level.

I told him that even though I hadn't looked thoroughly at his business, I doubt that I could find high correlation between any customer experience scores and loyalty for his business. After all where would disaffected customers go? Back to warming their homes with firewood? His response was that he wanted to build a company that customers want to do business with, and not a company they have to do business with. Of course, he had other motivations. One was that he didn't think the market conditions would persist as they were. Secondly, he was diversifying his business and venturing into the smart home space which is sure to be a more competitive space and he very much wanted to be able to leverage the existing relationships with his customer base.

As I got to know him he shared a letter he received from a customer so frustrated with his service that he went to great lengths and expense to move out of his service area. That letter troubled and inspired him to think more deliberately about his customer experiences and a future not driven by fear of deserting customers but of a future where customer experience is a differentiator.

Even in ultra-competitive industries, well-intending executives have always been reticent to paying really close attention to the customer experience, especially when there are costs involved. I was in a budget meeting many years ago and one executive asked us without smiling, "what would happen if we just stopped answering the phones?" Before long there was pros and cons list, and thankfully the cons narrowly beat the pros. He then assured us that he was only kidding and that we have to answer all phone calls, but to do it at the very cheapest cost possible.

It was clear to me that we wanted to handle customer interactions at the lowest possible cost to the company, (even if it aggravates customers a bit) but it shouldn't be so bad that customers will show up with pitchforks to our corporate headquarters. Forward thinking executives have a differing viewpoint, they see the customer service experience not as a necessary evil, but instead, the heart of what they do.

How Did We Get Here?

Is it really any surprise that the prevailing charge of contact centers everywhere was providing customer service at the lowest cost possible? Let's go all the way back to the beginning of our profession. Remember that for most of the 19ᵗʰ century, all customer interactions happened face to face, and it wasn't a department per se. It wasn't until 1876 when the telephone was invented that things really began to change. Eighty years later, the call center was born as big multi-nationals wanted to apply the lessons learned from the industrialization process to customer service.

Their aim was to carve out a customer service department separate from the rest of the organization. This new department would deal with customer's problems and demands, making it an assembly line of sorts, where the work is repetitive with lower-level workers employed to handle the volume. Like a lot of our most modern technological advancements, call center technology eventually became more cost effective, allowing smaller companies to get in the game. With the cost and technological bar lowered, the call center went mainstream. From the very beginning, customer care was a cost center that needed to be contained.

In the chase of cost savings, domestic outsourcing became popular. Naturally, if you needed cheaper labor, why not go into cheaper markets? So it didn't take long for customer service outsourcing to go mainstream.

I happen to think outsourcing is a part of the customer experience tapestry. Of course, the first question to ask yourself is why are you outsourcing? If it's to save money, I have a follow up question, how much money? What do I mean by how much? Have you explored the full costs?

I had front-row tickets to the early international outsourcing trends and ran outsourced call centers both domestically and internationally for ten years I can tell you that not only are the savings exaggerated, but the woeful customer experiences were also exaggerated and the truth is far more nuanced. Having done this very thing twice, I can tell you that the savings projections never quite add up when you start including all of the costs involved.

Let me get very specific here. Suppose your fully loaded costs to answer a customer's call comes to $6.50 per call, and if you outsourced domestically you could do it at $6.00 per call. At a call volume of 1,000,000 calls a year, you save $500,000 a year.

If you stop there, then you are doing yourself a disservice. To really make a good comparison, you must introduce other metrics. For example, let's compare repeat call rates. In the same example, assuming you had avoidable repeat calls climb roughly 5 percent, this causes your savings to diminish to $380,000 per year. Now, you can stop there or you can keep going. Look at the delta between your transactional loyalty scores (whether that be NPS or another metric), and see if there is another hidden cost. If after going through this level of rigor you conclude that there is still net savings that are important to you, then by all means go for it.

As for the customer experience woes, I have not met a North American customer who didn't have reservations about calling a contact center overseas. There are real issues associated with this and yes, they are sometimes exaggerated, but that is certainly par for the course. Sure, there is no doubt that North American customers would much rather discuss their situations and problems with customer service representatives located in North America due to the poor experience of dealing with outsourced support, and *not solely because they are located overseas*. Often times, the the language barrier is a stand in for other frustrations.

There isn't an appreciable difference in the frustration level while speaking with a rep in North America who you can't understand because of poor speaking skills or a rep in India whose accent is hard for you to comprehend. My point is that it isn't the outsourcing that frustrates consumers, but the disjointed experience. When these outsourcing customer to service industry relationships are set up for success, meaning deployed in contact types where the overall probability for success is very high, these horror stories tend to be minimal.

Suppose you realize that it is not so much about the cost, maybe the savings aren't all that compelling Instead, running a contact center isn't a core competency or fundamental that you want to include as a part of your organization. You would rather focus on the actual product or service and let someone else run the support and customer service sector of your operation. Here is something to keep in mind if that is your stance on the issue. The customer experience is at the very core of your business since you are in the *customer* business. If you outsource part of that operation, you can still be very successful so long as you remain actively engaged.

Customers are still calling you and not the outsourcer, so does your outsourced customer service staff understand your customers? Or is it transactional for them. How much of your strategy do they understand, and are their hearts in it as much as yours is? To that end, I recommend having a control group internally to use as a benchmark. By all means outsource, but do leave a small team in place, so that you can empathize with your outsourcers and use the two models in comparison to each other. If you are serious about your customer experience, you cannot measure them strictly by metrics. You have to be an active participant. Outsourcing your customer care is more akin to hiring a nanny. Now, is the nanny going to be doing some of the heavy lifting? Sure! But at the end of the day, you are still the parent.

Changing the conversation, and putting in a structure that is centered around what is best for the customer before any other concern is a dialogue that you are going to need to have within your organization, and it won't be easy.

In God We Trust, All Others Bring Data

I was an invincible sophomore in college, I had a terrific girlfriend with a grownup job. Life was good. At least until she wanted to discuss our future, so we planned a meeting at our favorite spot in the student union. I stayed up late the night before, deep in thought, contemplating the different scenarios. In the end, I showed up to the student union with a printout of a cost benefit analysis to help us decide the next steps in our relationship. To my chagrin, she stormed off and stopped taking my calls — she didn't even stay to hear the end of my analysis. I have been known to take this trust in data thing too far, it's a life mantra of sorts. I have to be reminded that data has its limits, particularly in human relationships.

Years later, I began a career in a contact center with a group of people who loved data as much as I do, I was home! By the way, I would like to start a petition to have a statue of the great Dr. Edwards Deming in front of every contact center. If only for his quote, "in God we trust, all others bring data".

No one measures everything quite like a contact center, and since most of its costs is associated with labor, when I say "everything" I actually mean its people. I think The NSA can learn a thing or two from the data collection that most contact centers collect on its frontline representatives.

I read a review on Glassdoor from a current employee about a local contact center. The headline was, **"homeless drug addicts have more freedom than Call Center Reps"**. I wanted to disagree or get defensive about everything that followed, but I found myself agreeing that most of the comments on the review were fairly typical. The working conditions accurately describe most call or contact centers. We track and measure our every move of our employees.

The mismatch here is that today, the charge for contact centers has changed but they are still run with a 90s mentality of low trust and a constant search for data to wring out more and more widgets. There was a time when all anyone looked to the contact center for was to crank out as many widgets as cheaply as possible and prevent customers from showing up at corporate with pitchforks. The contacts were repetitive and easy, they were routine status checks, payment requests, and general information contacts.

In case you haven't noticed, more and more of the mindless contacts (payments, status checks) are being handled by robots (automated systems, website, etc). In the past, when most customer inquiries were routine, metrics like average handle time (AHT) and rigid checklist metrics made sense. Now contacts that arrive for employees to handle are increasingly complex and no longer about handling more and more in cheaper ways but about building loyalty. Today more than ever, we do not need metrics that signal to employees that we do not trust them or are more concerned with cranking out more widgets.

Another popular mantra I heard was, "if you can't measure it you can't manage it". The industry adopted this maybe a little too literally, actually I am certain that we did! This guiding philosophy is micromanagement on steroids. We seem to measure everything to the microsecond, including the amount of time our employees spend on break, how many calls were transferred or put on hold, and the rate of speech. More and more experts are pontificating on whether the world of business may have gone too far with metrics, but that would be a topic in and of itself, certainly for another time and place.

The contact center is fixated on productivity and efficiency metrics above all else, while customer experience measurements are typically placed on the back burner, even when you look at most of the quality monitoring programs which tend to be loaded with a lot of *efficiency targets* like call control, the amount of time that the customer is on hold, etc. There is a rational explanation for this obsession with productivity. In a lot of organizations, the contact center is viewed as a cost center that has to be gutted every fiscal year. In other organizations the charge is more nuanced, and the mindset is to do more with less, *increase efficiency*—whichever way it is described, the bottom line is the *bottom line*.

There are few organizations that do not have this view and in fact are building their customer base primarily through the contact center (Zappos comes to mind). To illustrate this on my tour there years ago, I was struck by the fact that they recognized an employee with a call of over nine hours, and on their website they recognized another four hour call which was their longest call at the time. I suspect the vast majority of organizations operate their contact center differently, otherwise Tony Hsieh wouldn't be such an exception. Personally, I don't make value judgments in the different approaches In the end every organization has to decide the strategic role its contact center plays within the greater organization structure and then build on that model from there.

Given that the cost savings mandate is a reality for most, sound contact center leadership involves a constant re-engineering process with the technology to deliver on that charge. Since most of the contact center's overall costs are tied up in human resources, most of the bigger initiatives are designed to reduce compensation costs, whether it is reducing contacts or to handle the same contacts with fewer resources. In accomplishing the latter, handing every frontline employee with a figurative stopwatch to look at as they handle customer contacts may seem like a harmless idea. After all no one is saying that we should just shove the customer off the phone. It's okay to have longer calls, so long as there are plenty of shorter calls to reach your average. After all, we balance this goal with quality assurance so again, no harm done.

This line of thinking from within the contact center industry has been a part of our DNA for so long that many years ago, when I barely suggested removing AHT from the frontline employee's scorecard to my leadership team, you'd have thought I was suggesting we go on a baby punching spree.

My view is that given the modern customer expectations standards, customer loyalty is becoming more and more the charge for the contact center, and a lot of frontline employee scorecards now include customer satisfaction elements. To address this new shift, we still need to modify the scorecard even more, so the goals aren't conflicting – AHT must die!

In the context of customer experience, there are obvious reasons why the stopwatch (AHT) is harmful, and probably the biggest danger is that your employees will in fact hit this number you have set and hurt you in two significant ways. The first and most obvious way is in CSAT (or customer loyalty), for which the stopwatch approach can drive bad behaviors that negatively impact the customer experience. Frontline employees can get very creative in hitting this target, and still hit all the notes on your QA evaluation form. Take for instance if your customer says, "you know what, it will take a while for me to find my wallet to make this payment". If your rep has had many long calls already, my bet is they will politely provide your customer with your hours of operation and assure them that someone else will be happy to help at that time. If your goal is customer satisfaction, then there is absolutely nothing wrong with that interaction. If on the other hand you want loyal customers, opportunities like this to build the brand by going above and beyond are like gold—you can't have the stopwatch, as you should instead, want to free your employees to insist, "I don't mind holding, I know the feeling take your time, I will wait".

The second way this can hurt you is in FCR (first contact resolution). If more of your staff take shortcuts or are too focused on getting it done faster, you end up with higher repeat calls, which in the end drives up your operating costs. In the age of the consumer where the customer experience is so important, making this shift allows you to deliver something very critical that your consumers want (FCR) more consistently. Almost no other metric will move your CSAT score more than delivering resolution on the very first contact – not shorter wait times and not lower ASA. Put simply, you want loyal customers and you want to resolve their issues the first time. One surefire way to do that is to take a sledgehammer to the stopwatch. The best part of this approach is that as an added bonus, you can directly impact the bottom line by eliminating repeat calls.

Let me say without equivocation that I believe the charge to do more with less isn't going anywhere, and thus, the problem isn't that we are measuring AHT. Au contraire, it has more to do with whom you are measuring. I recommend first removing AHT from your frontline staffs' scorecard and instead leaving it on your site managements' scorecard. Secondly, develop a Voice of the Customer program (More on this in Part Three) system that is robust enough to address AHT in a customer experience context. This will be a case of *who you measure* being as important as *what you measure*. Think about how your management team tends to manage AHT. I suspect it is by printing an ACD report and attaching a note to it that says, "please bring your average handle time down" or by having a meeting that is centered around general tips that in the end the employee hears, "get the customer off the phone faster" and in most cases they do, with unintended consequences. If your frontline employees do not have an AHT target, your management teams have no choice but to take a holistic approach.

Consider telling your frontline team that you are more concerned with CSAT and that efficiency is still important, but not to the extent that it impacts the customer experience, and that in fact the inefficiencies you want to tackle are those that negatively impact the customer experience. The charge for your frontline leadership is therefore that they find outliers and customize the coaching and feedback on an individual level. The net result if done correctly is that AHT actually comes down the right way, much faster (without the repeat call side effects) because your frontline employees are no longer handed the stopwatch. They are given practical tips on how to perhaps navigate the systems faster, or conversation topics to avoid, or taught conversation transitional phrases and above all else, are coached in the context of improving the customer experience.

Once you operationalize this, the next level is even better. In my experience, what you find are some pretty interesting nuggets that you can begin to tease out by using data and input from your management team. Could higher AHT by some frontline employees be a net positive? Do they add more value (increased sales or CSAT scores and low customer call back rate) than what they spend in lower productivity? Could some of the most efficient reps who are helping bring down your AHT be net negatives? Is it also possible that you may come to find out that some of your *star employees* have customer interactions that feel transactional and result in missed sales opportunities, repeat contacts, and low customer satisfaction? Would your frontline management be better at addressing outliers with higher AHT? For example, there might be employees who haven't mastered the art of call control or those whose attempt to build rapport is ineffective. You can begin the process of pointing out this false choice of efficiency vs. effectiveness, or productivity vs. customer experience as there is a balance that keeps both sides happy.

Service Levels

One of the critical decisions in building liberating structures is around what access you are going to provide to your customers. Where can they reach you, when, and how long of a wait they can expect for a response. The first thing to consider is why customers are contacting you in the first place. If you do not understand this component, likely, none of the others will matter. Be very careful in answering that question. Put yourself in your customers' shoes to answer this. Journey map the customers' path to contacting you for help to understand clearly why they contact you in the first place. When you have that question answered in a broad sense, try answering it more specifically.

As an example, let's say that you are an online retailer who realizes that customers contact you for three reasons. One, because there are delivery issues or two, because there are product issues and three, because there are website issues. You can then expand upon those basic start points from there. Equally important as understanding why customers contact you, is understanding their feelings and emotions around those contacts. For instance, if you sell baby monitors, one reason a customer may call is because they are defective. This triggers you to develop some instant insight that helps you deliver a contextual experience. You now realize that the caller is unlike most callers in that they are likely a sleep deprived new parent, and needs assistance with their issues in the worst way. This is insight that you can begin to develop that will set you apart from your competition.

Now that you are very clear on what motivates your customers' interaction we can begin to draw up a customer access strategy so you know what they call about and why. You can now make some decisions on where you will serve up these interactions. In other words, you can now map each of these contacts and decide whether it should be handled online or over the phone. Your customer should not have to choose which channels to use, that's your job. There are tools that can make this process easier.

Visit http://amastenumah.com/the-curated-experience/   for more
information.

Service Level Goal

Service level targeting is a much-litigated topic, worthy of further discussion. There are a few schools of thought on this topic, but they all end up within a few yards of each other. Everyone faced with setting service level for the voice channel essentially ends up asking the same question, - "what do other call centers do? Or they benchmark in their industry and ultimately end up in the same place as everyone else in groupthinkville. So what should your service level be? This decision should be made based on your personal brand.

For starters, I bet you probably spend an inordinate amount of time worrying about customer wait time. While overly long wait times can be a driver of dissatisfaction, the truth is that customers don't mind *some* wait time - there is a sweet spot. You need to find the window of wait where your customers prefer to live. The trick is finding that sweet spot. I have plotted wait times and customer loyalty metrics and have found a very weak relationship. The other day I went to a grocery store that I frequent to buy shrimp. When I got there, I got in line and waited my turn. When I made it to the counter, I asked for two pounds of shrimp and was stopped by the owner as I was headed for the cashier. He asked, "what do you think?", and after he noticed the puzzled look on my face he said, "the lines are shorter now". He went on to brag about his hiring and training of staff, specifically in reducing wait times for his customers, for which I complimented him for his efforts.

The truth is that too many customer experience enhancement efforts like the one mentioned above involve a lot of resources, but do not improve customer loyalty. The reason for this is that they are put together based on bad information. When looking at the case of my local grocer, while it was nice of them to improve my wait time by 45 seconds, it did nothing to improve my satisfaction with the store, and even worse I didn't even notice. If you have been responsible for customer wait times whether that be service levels at a contact center, or at a brick and mortar store, you know how expensive even marginal improvements can be.

Before you commit resources to improve wait times, here are three questions you should ask yourself:

1. How big of an issue is your current wait time? Asking customers if they would like shorter wait times is no way to find the answer to this question. Be more deliberate, for example, ask customers for their feelings about current wait times, and then measure its relative importance to their loyalty. If your wait time is objectively too long, it will be apparent not only in customer feedback but in other customer behaviors. The question is where is the point of diminishing returns?

2. What will be the ROI of this reduction? When your wait time is 30 minutes, reducing it to two minutes has an obvious payoff. But what is the payoff from two minutes to 45 seconds? Do your customers even care?

3. What is the opportunity cost for this enhancement? Sure you can now brag about how quickly you respond, but what if you spent those resources on a topic that is more critical to your customers?

The bottom line is that you should most certainly fix chronic wait times. But before trying to eliminate all wait times, make sure at the very least, your customers will notice and they will become more loyal to you as a result. For someone who is familiar with the cost of improving the last mile or the last few seconds, make sure it is worth the investment. I use wait time as an example simply because it is very relatable, but you can use this yardstick for other metrics as well.

Remember, not all wait is created equal. If you have a technology that enables callback (or that holds the customer's place in line), the customer's tolerance for wait is different.

When I walk into a contact center, I would often ask what their call service level goal is and the answer is almost always "we answer 80 percent of calls within 10 or 20 seconds". Now on the surface that sounds great, until you dig further and realize that they are looking at a monthly service level number, which means that you could stink up the joint for 22 of the 30 days in the month and still be hitting the scorecard. Now imagine you are a customer of this company, and that most days in any given month, your wait time was astronomical, but internally the company has no plans to fix it because they see that nothing is broken as they are hitting their goals.

If you go look even further at an intra-day level, on any given day, you are answering calls immediately in one half hour and customers are waiting 45 minutes the next, sure there is volatility in call arrival patterns. Many of these calls have a very predictable volatility pattern, and it takes work to solve the yo-yo effect, but the advantage is that you have a wait time expectation that customers can trust and one that is meaningful. I recommend you set a different kind of service level that measures how many half hour intervals you hit within a given time period. For example, if you are open daily from 8:00 to5:00 p.m., you should measure success as how many of the 18 intervals that you reached service level.

These are the building blocks for creating liberating structures, but the core of every building block should be focused on putting the needs of the customer first. It's about understanding who your customers are, what expectations they have of you, and how to create an environment that is efficient but liberating for your customer experience goals.

Part Two
Empowered People

Fire All Your Employees

I was sick with food poisoning after a visit to a fast food restaurant. When I was well enough, I contacted them and they offered me help in the form of a coupon for more of their food. I thought the company was callous, because they claimed that this was all they could do. Your company has a face, a human face. For McDonalds, it's the employee at the drive-thru or behind the counter. For Zappos.com, it's the voice of the representative behind their toll free number. For Southwest Airlines, it's the flight attendant. While your company can feel like an existence on paper when customers interact with your company, it is very much a human interaction with the face of your company. So if you have the view that people are a part of the ingredients for success but that it should be the cheapest possible people, then you may be treading on treacherous waters.

There will be fewer employees in customer experience in the not too distant future. Data driven technology (which we will cover later) is driving this trend. In fact, there will be less employees period. When you do decide to utilize humans it better be because they are needed and will add value. You also need to value what they bring, if you don't by all means fire them all and put machines in their place. You will be doing your customers a favor. There will still be plenty of places where a human interaction is necessary or a value add. Often times you want your organization to have a face or a voice, and looking for the cheapest possible face is not a winner.

Over time, you save lots of money on labor costs, and the labor you get, by saving money is helping to devalue the face of your organization and you end up with a face that is indifferent and apathetic. It is a tall order to expect your technology or structures to carry the load. I think creating a great customer experience program rests with people – great people! The school of thought that technology or structures will make the human part of this moot is not one I subscribe to. The notion that you can dumb down the job of building relationships with your customers so much so that the skills involved is no higher than doing fast food prep is not one I agree with. Consider this, it is harder to get employed at Southwest Airlines as a baggage handler much less a customer facing employee, than it is to get into Harvard Business School. They believe the right employee makes all the difference – and in an industry where almost everyone else is losing money or angering customers, they are profitable and creating raving fans. I am philosophically aligned with their thinking. Don't get me wrong, I think there are two other parts to delivering a great experience – liberating structures (which we covered earlier) and data driven technology, but let me be clear, your employees are the most important piece of the experience.

Before you start making names *of people to fire* list with visions of poaching Southwest Airline employees to take their place, let's take a minute to look inward. Let's put your onboarding and training through some scrutiny and then turn our attention to hiring.

Training and Orientation

Fifteen years ago, I was a young software developer with a half-baked product and dreams of making it big. I started gaining a little traction and had a big lead, so I put on my oversized suit I purchased from Burlington Coat Factory and knocked on the door of a local call center. A lady named Tracy welcomed me – she had dreamy blue eyes and a Texas drawl that sounded like music to my ears. I pitched my game changing software. It was a voice recognition program and she seemed genuinely interested in the possibilities and politely told me she would hand my materials to her bosses. In retrospect, she must have realized that I was closer to starvation than to a billion dollar software company because she would call me days later to talk me into a position as a telemarketing sales associate.

When it was time for orientation and training, I noticed that it was set up like every typical company. We were shown slides of the company's beginnings that was very much inside out. We learned about the great company founder and his dreams to have everyone in America have credit card insurance. Soon enough, we started learning about credit card insurance and why our company's flavor of credit card insurance is the very best ever. Then it went on to rally us for one cause lining our pockets and lining the company's pockets with cold hard cash. Very little time was spent on the customers' needs, aspirations, and desires.

From that day forward, every employee's mindset was framed from that. My job was about helping *our* company grow – our products and services are awesome and anyone in front of me should want them. I walked out of orientation very clear on what my mission with the company was – separate customers from their wallets. Your orientation is probably not much different from my example, and this inside-out view, is not a good thing.

I would propose an alternative, an outside-in view. One in which the customer is at the very center, so that if you were in the wedding gown business, the center of the show should be a woman who is about to get married. Her thoughts, her feelings and emotions as she plans her big day will be front and center. You would show new employees how big this day really is and how important it is to her that everyone does their part, not to make the company more profits, but to make her day special. Culminating in the fact if they make her day special, the company will do very well. Setting the tone in this way ensures that everyone is clear on what the focus of the company will be. This message empowers and motivates your people to go out and deliver the kinds of experiences you want to be known for.

If you have spent many hours in training rooms like I have, you probably don't associate many positive adjectives to them. A lot of trees have died on the topic of training, but indulge me with a few words on this topic. Have you been through your training rooms recently and do you think anyone really retains much of the content? If you have a great training program, it is delivered via e-learning or in person with role-play sprinkled in, and it engages its participants. If you have a bad training program, it is a snooze-fest interrupted with meaningless knowledge retention tests. Even if your program is of the former, training is still only designed to prepare your reps on the scientific components of customer experience; how to utilize systems, new product rollouts, rote tasks, etc. It still fails woefully at improving what is really going to differentiate your experience – those elements are more art than science. For example, if you are in the business of telling customers *no* on occasion, there is a deliberate art to doing that without denigrating your customer experience. Your people can be empowered to do this, and that is a skill that is imparted via coaching and not training. You could introduce the concept via training, but to really get proficient at the art, an individualized coaching program is paramount. You have to in almost real-time, with the full context of what comes naturally to the individual rep and a real life scenario in hand, deliver feedback that is impactful.

Even if you upgrade your training program and onboarding process, don't forget that someone still has to be charged with nurturing these professionals—they are your frontline leaders. If people are the most important ingredient to create personalized experiences, the most important group of people on your experience team are your frontline leaders. I have seen success in spite of middle managers but never seen success in spite of terrible frontline managers. They are more critical than your frontline employees, for one thing they hire, and develop those frontline employees, even the best frontline employees will falter under bad leadership.

Don't Try This at Home and The Impact of Top Notch Leaders

About a decade ago, my boss told me that I was going to be taking over one of the most underperforming teams in the enterprise. Inwardly, I wanted no part of it. I was new at managing frontline leaders and was just getting my team in shape. I told him that I would love to explore the opportunity. I took home their metrics and as I reviewed it, I was apoplectic. They were historically bad. Though my boss told me that while the supervisors were decent, they had really bad agents on their team because the shifts were undesirable. I had a different perspective and in my mind it all fell on the shoulders of the leaders. I knew the only way to impact change was to make changes at the leadership level and get the attention of the leaders with the goal of upgrading their play. As I prepared to meet with them, I thought of ways I could encourage them, but the more I looked at their performance, the madder I got. So I scrapped that plan, I decided instead to give them a wakeup call. On the day of the meet and greet, my boss gathered all of the frontline leaders in a conference room. He then introduced and yielded the floor to me. I began by saying, "congratulations to all of you, what you have accomplished here is quite remarkable, you all should be very proud." There was some nervous laughter in the room and in retrospect, I wished I just stopped there and went into my plan on how we turn the ship around but I couldn't help myself. I went on to tell them that being that bad required talent. I said you don't deliver these kinds of numbers by indifference, the only way to be this bad is to intentionally want to be bad and work really hard at being terrible. I am shocked that my boss didn't fire me on the spot. He was mortified and I almost lost all the managers.

Despite my failed attempt at inspiration, the team went on to start performing at the very top within weeks. The approach I used is not one I would use again, because I had to do a lot of damage control with half of the group who had real potential. I am just as convinced as I was there that your frontline leadership roles should be where you should be the least compromising – you want the very best and nothing less.

There's a lot of research on the impact that leaders make at the top but when you're in the business of customer expectations, your frontline leaders by and large have to be A players or you don't have a shot. You have to be uncompromising on this point. There's no room for mistakes.

I Would Rather Flip Burgers

I managed a contact center where the attrition rate was close to 200 percent. It gets worse. There was a McDonalds in the same parking lot that paid 25 percent less and routinely poached employees from us. They had significantly better employee retention numbers than we did and to be frank, it bugged the heck out of me. With apologies to McDonalds, I thought my value proposition was better. So as we dug into the problem, it really came down to this – we hired the wrong people, and to a lesser extent we did a lot of wrong things after that. So we brought human resources, training, and operations together to solve the problem.

The focus of the people doing the hiring was to look at the job qualifications and to hire the best qualified candidates. The problem was that qualifications, like education, and years of experience are good first steps, but if you use those and generic interview questions as the basis for hiring, you will end up where we were – in an unacceptable rate of attrition. Suppose a freshly minted computer science college graduate walks into the room wanting an entry level job. You pay significantly below what people with this candidate's degree earns. Should you hire this candidate? Suppose another applicant comes in without a college degree, but has done an average of eight month stints for two other contact centers, are they a good candidate? It depends on the interview and that was the point of the intervention.

What you can create are questions that target the very attributes that are critical to success for you, weighted to importance, then begin to calibrate those scores to the performance of your reps in production. What you end up with is a predictable model for picking talent to place within your organization. Keep refining this process, time and time again and you will be in good shape in terms of hiring.

When it comes to hiring I don't think you need to reinvent the wheel, but you do need to make this a little more science than art. If you look at your existing populace, there are model employees, and you often joke about cloning them. I think it is very much worth the investment to explore ways to end up with these model employees more times than not. One way that I have found particularly useful in accomplishing this is by figuring out the criteria you look for in a successful employee for your organization. I would document a list of these criteria and weigh them by importance. Now figure out how to use the interview and other screening mechanisms to measure said criteria, then do a regression analysis comparing screening scores to their actual performance. If you tweak this every four months or so, you will get a lot better at ending up with the right people.

For more help on this, visit: http://amastenumah.com

Remote Agents

You may have heard that remote contact center agents outperform brick and mortar counterparts and you may have heard different reasons for why this is the case. I'm here to give you a view from someone who has deployed this multiple times and has the bruises to prove it. Speaking of my bruises, let me share with you about my first foray into this space. I had the opportunity to join a team that was expanding our footprint above and beyond the brick and mortar centers into the work from home space. This was at a time when the remote contact center agent industry was still taking shape. My job was to build a 300-agent strong program, and it was a fun ride at times but more often than not I was inadvertently creating a long list of what not to do when building a work from home program.

Our approach was from a place of hubris and as such, we had a lot of assumptions that didn't pan out. Our premise was that working from home was the greatest thing to happen to contact center agents and therefore all agents should feel privileged to be a part of it. And so we created stringent eligibility criteria so we would end up with only the best and the very brightest on this team. The thinking was that only those with demonstrated success in our brick and mortar facility were worthy – this was the wrong assumption. To further stack the deck, we furnished them equipment from their desktop to their headset – only the best for our elite agents. The thinking was that we would collect them upon their departure (this turned out to be foolish as we lost more hardware than our most pessimistic forecasts).

Our assumption that there will be a net uptick in performance by having people work remotely also turned out to be false, in fact net performance went down. To be fair some agents went home and set the world on fire, but by and large, some stayed the same and some even got worse. The blended result was a net decline. Another assumption was that attrition was also dramatically lower, this also proved to be wrong. Sure it was a little bit better than the mean which was disappointing considering the fact we only allowed the best of the best to work from home. I could go on, but

I dwell on some of the missteps and faulty assumptions because over a decade has passed and I still see some of these mistakes in the marketplace.

Before you get the wrong idea, I am a big proponent of remote agent programs and it actually makes sense for a lot of organizations. I have had a chance to build the program again after my first foray and fortunately I also know what success looks like. You need to be clear on why you are doing this, as for some it is business continuity, for others it is cost savings, expansion, or expanding your geographical radius for recruiting purposes to name a few. Regardless of your motivation, the two most popular forms of building these programs are the telecommute agent and the true remote agent models. The difference by and large is that in the remote agent model, the agent never comes to a brick and mortar facility to work and therefore has a very wide radius. The model with the biggest payoff is the remote agent model but as you may suspect, it is also more challenging to execute. I'll focus most of my thoughts on the remote agent opportunity as I think the telecommute model has a limited upside, but the learnings cut across both models.

The first thing to do is to begin to view it as a completely different beast from your brick and mortar programs. If you do not plan on devoting a lot of time and resources to building or buying a good remote workforce program then you should not proceed. A thrown together remote agent program will do some good around the margins, but overall it will be a distraction. One of the most common reasons people decide to get in this space is a way to efficiently expand their footprint (whether it is to add seats or because you have outgrown your current geographic market). Nothing else expands your operations better than remote agent or home shoring.

There are countless studies that tell you how much better the performances of home agents are compared to brick and mortar. I can tell you that in programs that are built correctly, the performance is absolutely better than brick and mortar. Despite what some remote agent practitioners will have you believe, the reason for this uptick in performance is not because they work from home. The real reason you get this group of high performing people is that you get far more selective in your hiring because you have dramatically expanded your recruiting radius. Consider this, imagine you have a contact center in Omaha, Nebraska and you can recruit within a 40 mile radius of your location. All of a sudden you just added more applicants to your pool by a factor of 100 by now hiring in ten states.

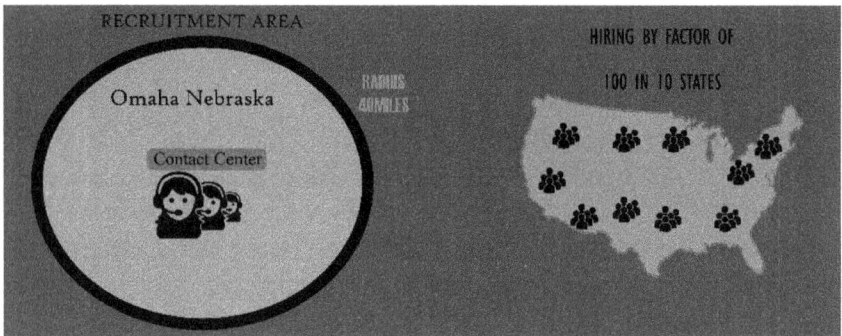

You now attract far more applicants than you used to so you can be more selective. This can fill your team with the very best. College grads, who will not drive to your shop will work for the same pay at home and retirees who have had successful careers will also head your way. These teams routinely outperform brick and mortar. Not because being in their own home brings out the best in them, but because you can rig the game by picking a team with more A players. In the end you want a team – the right team of empowered people, and if you expand your recruiting radius, your odds of finding them dramatically increases.

I think most organizations struggle with brick and mortar training but virtual training for customer experience agents is a whole other animal. Putting lipstick and heels on your PowerPoint slides and putting it on a webinar isn't going to do the trick. You are going to need to deliberately redesign your training tools in such a way that it allows engagement with the participants. You should certainly utilize the old-faithful, self-paced, instructor-led approach with video technology to ensure the reps on the other end aren't also watching a show on Netflix to stay awake.

You are also going to need to hire some help if you do not have the skill set on your team to do this, as even the best brick and mortar trainers often make terrible trainers in the virtual world. A lot of their tricks and tips are created for a brick and mortar classroom. After you have built a good virtual training program, you can also simulate virtual training in your brick and mortar shop by hiring agents and bringing them into a site (the reason you do this is the safety of still having the brick and mortar available in case you need to revert). Then have them sit in isolated individual cubicles with higher walls. You then conduct your virtual training and begin to identify gaps within your process, with the security of being able to roll back if you need to. Then measure the outcome to see what is working and what needs work.

To build an empowered remote agent workforce, another place to put a lot of focus on is on-going support as you absolutely cannot copy and paste your brick and mortar support and expect it to work in a virtual world. You are going to need to re-think your support structures for them. Imagine one of the agents in your facility walks up to a supervisor to ask a question and when she gets there she sees that her supervisor is helping another rep. Chances are, she will probably wait her turn and get her issues answered. Now imagine your reps waiting for support from home where they do not have the benefit of seeing what the supervisor is doing and as such, a one minute wait feels like 20 minutes. If you plan to provide the same level of support for your remote agents, you will leave them frustrated. You are going to need to rethink the channels you use and the service levels you set. My standard is to provide higher service levels for your reps than you do your best customers. In terms of channels, instant messaging and phone calls are two of the most effective channels. However you decide to set up your support, speed is key and tolerance for wait is very low.

When it comes to equipment, there are different models but the most effective is having your employees provide their own core equipment (PC/laptop/tablet), supplemented by you providing accessories like headsets. You then utilize software to serve as gatekeepers to validate whether or not their equipment meet the minimum standard every time they logon, checking everything from internet speeds to software and hardware. It can also tell them what parts of the criteria they didn't pass so they can self-cure. For example if there are viruses on the computer it will prompt the employee to take curative measures. In the age of gigabit speeds, you should be pretty prescriptive on what speeds they should get. You should get connected with ISPs and be versed on what offerings are available so that you can ensure quality of service for your voice calls.

Engagement

"My goal is to be President of the United States", I had to read it one more time to be sure, after all this was supposed to be a self appraisal by someone on my staff that works in our call center. I found myself immediately passing judgment, I wondered if she was serious. I internally began to mock her ambition. In fact I laughed out loud. Fortunately, I came to my senses and spoke with her as an adult. As it turns out, she was not delusional, she had dreams. I offered to help her on her journey, even though it had no benefit to my company or me. She stayed on for years and was one of my top performers. You want a culture that encourages leaders to selflessly advocate for their employees.

If your idea of employee engagement is ordering food, then you are in trouble especially if they are remote. If you now have geographically dispersed employees, buying some boxes of pizza and throwing them on the counter and calling it engagement is not going to work remotely. You are going to have to be far more deliberate in the way you organize your engagement activities. For starters, you'll need to be more personal and you are going to need individual level data via things like surveys to understand employee preferences. Then you can overlay that with programs that have near universal appeal. Specifically in the area of meaning, doing meaningful work drives almost all of your employees, and figuring out how to make that connection is the biggest incentive you can offer. I can tell you from experience that enlisting your customers is an effective way to accomplish this. Many organizations share customer notes that talk about the actions a rep took but you can go one step further to highlight the impact it had on their lives. Begin to change the conversation, zoom out for your employees from handling interactions to enriching lives in meaningful ways. Making this connection should be front and center in your engagement strategy for both a brick and mortar and remote workforce.

You are Going to Need Coaches

It was like clock-work. At 8:30 she will come by my desk and put a highlighted sheet of paper on it. I was a new frontline sales rep doing my best to get up to speed, and every morning without fail my supervisor would walk around with a printout of everyone's performance from the prior day and hand out copies to each team member. Then once a week she met with everyone individually, and when it was my turn she handed me the sheet with my name highlighted and said, "you are new but you need to start making sales, because right now you are not where we want you to be". I thought to myself, "no kidding". She then went on to say, "I would like to see your numbers go up". And I kept thinking "me too". She ended with saying, "I will check in periodically to see if you are improving". She then threw in, "you can do it", and asked me to call in her next victim.

I didn't quite see the point of this method of coaching. She provided no *how-to*, all she did was state where I was and where she would like me to be, sprinkled some faux motivational phrases in the middle, and ended it there. I wasn't hitting goals, I knew it and so did she. I knew how much farther behind I was after I saw it in print, but still didn't know how to stop the bleeding.

Whether you have employees in your building or working remotely, you need to develop them. Most coaching sessions tend to be backward looking, in fact they often occur when an employee has screwed up. The type of coaching that is impactful is forward-looking coaching or situational coaching, coaching that occurs purposefully in almost real-time, tailored to the needs of the individual. For example, you have identified that a cause of pain for your customers exists on calls where you have to say *no*. Maybe you have cracked the code on how you can frame *no* and still make customers feel good about the interaction. On the job coaching of the individual, during the call or seconds after they just had one of these calls is the way to go, not during their next week's coaching sessions.

Coaching that is about the future, and about the individual's needs and not the generic trends gleaned from a report
will make the difference in the end. In the battle of hearts and minds of customers, the organizations that win are the ones who get the art of customer connections right. To achieve this, they will utilize coaching to create an army that is adept at resolving customer issues but more importantly, deliver personalized experiences that are superior to the competition.

Crowducation

As your agents begin to talk to customers, they constantly have questions and by and large they ask these questions to their leaders and peers over and over again. In good organizations, some of these questions and answers are already documented in a knowledgebase or at least have a vehicle to update it. It usually has a cute name or acronym. Some are powered by homegrown software, SharePoint, or one of the knowledge management systems in the market.

You tend to have a handful of people in your organization who are the only ones trusted to provide instructions to your reps. The thinking is, if you let anyone else update the knowledgebase, anarchy will reign. If you look around your center, you have probably noticed that your agents seek each other's assistance quite often for answers. We need to remember that there are informal leaders on the street, who not only love to help but also are quite good at it. The problem is, they feel in conflict with your content manager. This is the group that writes the stiff FAQs and *how-to* manual that is never completely up to date because your business is constantly changing. Furthermore no one wants to read most of the content they write, it is written as though your company is a law firm, sure it is free of spelling and grammatical errors but it is also free of life and zest. Have you looked at the age and online behavior of your audience? Well, let me save you some time. At home, they Google questions they have and when they get the answers they are often written in conversational language by the crowd. Then the crowd edits the answers over and over again for accuracy, votes up and down the most helpful, and it works spectacularly well. This same approach can work in your own center.

How do you apply this in your contact center to unleash and empower your people? Well, what you do is utilize existing technology to enable this. What you want is to leverage your existing knowledgebase to enable the *crowducation* of your team. You create the *Yahoo Answers* model internally. Your reps ask questions and other reps answer them. Then you store this question and answer so that the next person who has a similar question can see the question and see the most appropriate answer. You can *gamify* it as well by rewarding answerers with badges, identifying your most active participants, and if you are a control enthusiast, you can further vet the answers Otherwise you let them post to the same knowledgebase.

You can start by utilizing this to augment your knowledgebase and over time it can replace more and more of the articles people aren't crazy about reading. Suppose your rep has a question about how to process a past due payment. They would likely search, "how do you process a past due payment?". Instead of only a stodgy knowledgebase article, you could put that on the left and put a crowd-based answer on the right. An educated decision can then be made based on the most popular answer available.

There is another level to take this to. There is a lot of work being done in many organizations to connect the CRM and knowledgebase by putting them side by side and adding some intelligence. The best use case I have seen is building a knowledge management system that is integrated with your CRM that predicts what piece of information your reps will need next. Say your rep is looking at a past due customer, key pieces of information related to dealing with past due accounts is presented as job aids without them having to search for it, as you already have all of the data in place that you need to serve up the information they may want to search for. Building this kind of intelligence into your knowledgebase and CRM is not technology for the future, it is already here and organizations have already been adding automation to handle some of the recommended actions.

Three years ago, one of my best reps was on the phone with a customer and it wasn't going very well. She was on the receiving end of unrelenting verbal accosting but she kept her cool, even though the customer pressed on. This culminated in the customer asking her who the vice president over customer service was and she calmly replied, *Joe Biden*. The five seconds of awkward silence following was pure joy. It stopped the customer in his tracks and she recovered and gave the customer my name and contact information. She turned the customer around, and pretty soon she convinced the customer that she was an advocate by telling her that I was actually visiting her office in Arkansas that week and she would personally make sure I heard about the troubles she had. She and her manager shared this story with me and we listened to the recorded call a couple of times, laughing and praising the masterful job she did.

I probably don't need to tell you that your frontline customer facing teams have some of the most difficult jobs in the organization. I also don't need to tell you how resilient and calm they are in the face of great challenges. I don't know if the job they have transitions them in this way or if they already had those qualities and then gravitated to the job. In either case, we should all be thankful for them. If you lead such a team you have a duty to improve their experiences on the frontline and you cannot focus on the customer without taking care of those who are charged with customer service.

I have no doubt you have asked a lot from them but for once let them do the asking, as it's your turn to serve them. Ask them how you can be helpful and you will get a laundry list of requests. So let's review what may be on that list and cover a few of the items.

I suspect that the list will include compensation, so do not ignore it. You can laud their efforts to the heavens, but it will fall on deaf ears if you are not fighting the good fight of trying to get them adequately compensated. This is no easy task you are not going to be getting a standing ovation when you go to your CFO asking for more money to invest in the frontline, especially if you work in an organization that views customer service as an assembly line. Every organization understands ROI, and that's where you come in. You can begin making the case for the revenue they generate and/save the company, the value of customer retention, and start taking bites at the apple. A good place to start is to simply get funding to reward your employees for helping to drive up your customer loyalty scores.

They are also going to ask you for your trust, for you to loosen the reins a little. This will take on different forms, but the ask is that you eliminate the checklists, eliminate everything that screams, "I don't trust you or your decision making". This includes overly prescriptive policies and metrics like AHT that give you a false sense of control but hurt the customer experience.

Lastly, there will be a lot of items that are about the customer - their customer. No one can better articulate the problem with your customer experience better than your frontline. Don't get me wrong, it is going to be painful for you to hear, but you need to hear all of it to help you prioritize where to start. Hopefully this book will give you ideas on how you might tackle them. Creating a curated customer experience is not something you can create with structures alone. You need the right people – empowered people. I need not remind you how high the stakes are on the journey of improving the experiences of your customers. To be effective, you should stop saying, "our representatives are the most important people in the company" when your actions say the opposite. Such empty words make things worse. Instead, focus on looking for ways you can empower them to be effective on the frontline. Live the principle of employee first, customer second.

Part Three
Data Driven Technology

Your Call is Very Important to Us

I was desperate enough to call Best Buy on the phone, and their automated system informed me that there was a long wait. I was disappointed but then shortly after that the system told me it could hold my place it line and call me back when I made it to the top of the queue, and it did! As a customer I loved it. I salivate at what is already possible today—specifically as it relates to improving the Customer Experience.

I get excited at the power of technology overall, but specifically in the customer experience field – the future looks bright. The question is how do we harness it to curate the best possible experience for customers? It is about intentionality, to stop seeing technology as simply a mechanism to make you more efficient.

Your mission if you are in CX is to combine information you have about the customer and your business with the power of technology to delight customers.

Curating experiences customer love involve three ingredients. We have talked about two of the three ingredients - liberating structures and empowered people. I saved data driven technology for last, because I started my career in technology and it's the most underutilized arsenal in your tool box. My goal is to get you started and give you ideas to get more creative in how you deploy technology.

Arguably one of the most underrated technological advancements of the last decade in CX is customer call back in lieu of hold, similar to what I experienced with Best Buy. Instead of customers waiting on hold, it holds their place in line for them and calls them back. Consumers generally love it, of course not as much as getting their calls answered promptly, but far better than forcing them to sit on hold and wait. There are a number of ways to implement this but be very clear on your goals before you do. If your only goal is to mitigate customer perceptions about your long wait times, it may be fairly straightforward for you.

The great news about this is that in every implementation I have seen, overwhelmingly, customers are big fans. They report lower effort scores and higher customer satisfaction numbers compared to waiting on hold. If you have objectives above and beyond that, say for example you want it to solve your staffing problem, then pay close attention. This may sound counterintuitive but it may not solve your staffing problem (if you have one) in fact it could exacerbate it. If you introduce this technology it will improve your customer experience but potentially compound your staffing problem. This happens because one of the side effects is that it can reduce real abandons, or put differently give you even more calls to answer. So if for example you are running occupancy of 90 percent, and abandons are 25 percent, adding this technology may make things worse for your staffing problem.

I ran operations where we only cared about improving the customer experience if it also demonstrably improved top or bottom line in the short term as well. Improving the experience for the *experiences sake* wasn't a luxury we had. So as I looked into this technology, I saw it as an opportunity to help operationally as well. What we were faced with were some very rough intervals, where volume was about five to six times the mean, and the need was to move some of the calls to other friendly intervals where the volume was lower than the mean. So to get a productivity bump out of virtual hold, we took a look at our rough intervals. The thinking was that while virtual hold will improve the customer experience by holding the customer's place in line, it does very little to solve the staffing problem, and it can even compound it as we discussed earlier. So instead, we created a new queue for customers who opted for virtual hold and then de-prioritized those calls. The key to making this seamless is the expectations set throughout the process with the customer and your agents. Be very clear with your customers on what will happen next. Give them options when you can and give them an opportunity to select their call back number as well as an estimated time for callback. It is critical that you bring your agents in on this and coach them on how to handle these calls in the most frictionless way possible. Ideally, you want the rep to start the call by acknowledging that this is a call back as there is no sense in pretending the customer hasn't been wanting to have this conversation for a while now.

Smart Transfer

I called the phone company to port my number to another carrier and cancel my services. After surviving IVR Hell, I was finally connected with a representative who promised to help, so I poured my heart out to her. Then of course, she tried to *retain* me as a customer, and I politely declined. She then offered to transfer me to "someone who can help". She waited on the line for the next rep to arrive, informing the next rep, "Mr. Tenumah would like to cancel his service", and then she wished me luck and hung up. Needless to say, I had to repeat my entire story even though I had at this point invested a total of 40 minutes on this transaction.

Most practitioners will tell you that warm transfers or warm handoffs are always better than cold transfers. They would usually make the argument without qualification. This assertion usually sounds good, after all who doesn't like the idea of warm transfers – the first representative listens to the customer's concerns attentively, determines they can't help the customer and then diligently relays that information to the next rep so the customers don't repeat themselves. I encourage you to listen to your warm transfer calls in practice. In most cases, the next rep is transferring just enough information to be dangerous about the customer's issue, furthermore it is tainted with third party biases and the net result is the customer having to re-tell their story once again because key details are left out, or the entire situation was lost in translation. Probably the most egregious part of this practice is the waste of resources, as it needlessly ties up two reps, thus elongating another customer's wait time. There is a better way.

I like to call it SmarTransfer. The goal is to utilize your employees and data driven technology to create a continuous conversation with your customers. What you want to do is to be effective and efficient, so you want your default setting as cold transfer but with these three guardrails. The first is to utilize technology to transfer all the call details over to the next representative seamlessly, including the account verification, account information, call notes, etc., all without the need of tying up two representatives. Secondly, ensure that everyone is coached on how to utilize the technology to make this effortless for the customer – invest in oversimplification! The third tip may be the most critical; ensure that all parties are clear on how this should work. Remember, for a transferred call to be considered part of a great customer experience, it has to be a continuous conversation. The customer should be prepped, and then the next agent must be coached on picking up the conversations, utilizing all the gathered information that has been transferred. To do this well, the initial rep should be coached to write the notes correctly, explicitly addressed to the next rep and not written like a note addressed to no one and everyone. The next rep should also be empowered to use good judgment to warm transfer as necessary, you need not be overly prescriptive on this last point, trust me they know.

To be clear, the goal should be to drive out transfers as much as possible, but there are ways to reduce the pain in the remaining transfers. While warm transfers sounds good, it ties up two agents and the experience is not necessarily better, and it can actually be a net negative.

IVR

Most customers are always looking for the most painless route to get what they need from companies they do business with. While automated systems can and do get a bad reputation, I have argued for years that automated systems (when built correctly) are usually easier than interacting with humans in many cases.

Recently, I drove to the bank. I passed right by the available tellers and instead waited in line to use the ATM to make the withdrawal I needed. Like you, I did this because the automated machine is superior to a teller in making a withdrawal of $50 from my checking account.

One of the best experiences I have had at a fast food chain occurred at an airport, where I could place my order on a touchscreen, pay and simply wait for my food to be delivered to me. At the heart of these choices lies a need to utilize the most painless route to interact with companies. This yearn is increasingly being met by smart data driven technologies.

Too many automated systems are built solely for the purpose of cost savings or contact deflection for the companies, and they often deliver those cost savings by frustrating the customer. Even among fellow customer experience practitioners, automated systems have a bad reputation. To me, the only automated systems worth building are ones customers will voluntarily choose over a human.

Here are three reasons why you should build data driven automated systems that customers prefer to humans:

1. Because it will actually increase customer loyalty. I hate to break it to you, but your customers aren't really dying to talk to you, what they want is to get their issue resolved via the least painful path. Identifying situations where that path involves more machine than human is exactly what your customers want. Customers are loyal to brands that make things easy and not only is smart automation a key part in that journey, in many instances it is superior to human interactions.

2. Because it will save you money. Automated systems built to the *easier than human* standard actually have the added benefit of saving you more over the long run. Customers will flock to it and utilization will go up without the pesky side effect of customer defection.

3. Because it will keep your employees happier. The truth is, handling the same routine tasks over and over again doesn't stimulate your employees. They would actually welcome some variety coupled with empowerment to fully utilize their skills. If your goal becomes resolving customer issues with as little customer effort as possible, you find that in many cases, it is data driven technology that is in a starring role.

Customers want their issues resolved in the most efficient manner, they do not hate automated systems, they hate bad automated systems. In the same way, they do not like unhelpful representatives who are not empowered.

Stop Interrogating Customers

I have used the same phone carrier for ten years, and even though that relationship is longer than many marriages, every time I call in about my account, I am thoroughly interrogated before they would even discuss the reason for my call.

I needed to add a new line to my mobile phone plan, so I started online and made my changes. I didn't get a confirmation, so I called customer service. First off, I went through IVR hell, (I'm generally pro self-service as I articulated earlier). After surviving that, I was then thoroughly interrogated by the phone rep, with the most vexing question being, "may I have your name please". Like the TSA, she was not letting me get to my reason for calling until she was done interrogating me. At the end of the ordeal, she assured me the changes were made and would be effective shortly. She then thanked me for being a "valued customer of over ten years". I felt neither valued nor like a customer. The next day I logged on, only to see the changes were not effective so I called back, only to again go through IVR hell, get interrogated by another rep, you get the idea.

Have you wondered why we have to verify information when we call in to make routine interactions? To put this differently, my cell phone provider is trying to protect me from someone who stole my phone, only to call customer service to see if plan changes are effective immediately or by the next billing cycle. I will tackle the fact that verifications by answering questions over the phone are a relic, and ineffective in protecting anyone in a bit. Even if you accept that these hurdles are necessary protections, do we need them on every interaction? Can't they be positioned at points in the interaction that feel more natural? If all I need is a response that is applicable to all customers, is an interrogation necessary? There's almost no value to anyone in these interrogations. If there is still a defense, it is that our security is at stake – or is it? What you tell yourself is that interrogations are the only way to authenticate the customer on the phone. There is a far better way to accomplish this task without an interrogation, data driven technology can help.

I am a rewards member at a local store. I can walk in, pick up thousands of dollars in merchandise, and go through the self-checkout lane without anyone getting in my way. If I get home and have a need to call that same national retailer, I would be thoroughly interrogated like a common criminal. On the surface, knowledge-based authentication has a way of making us feel safe. The theory is these are questions that only the customer would have answers to. That said maybe 20 years ago, no one would have ever known my mother's maiden name, but I surely don't need to convince you that a low level criminal with a dial up connection and a bit of patience can figure it out.

There are bad guys trying to gain access to customer accounts via the telephone, but burning down the house to solve a mice infestation problem has never been a good idea. Knowledge-based authentication is a relic. Consumers themselves on social media, data breaches, and hackers have now made the information we are verifying available to criminals. So if interrogations aren't keeping consumers, then what exactly are they doing? Interrogations annoy the heck out of customers, all the while the bad guys are gaming the system. The financial resources wasted on the interrogation is in hard dollars. Not to mention the hit to top line revenue will take as customers increasingly pick frictionless experiences in deciding whom to do business with.

I think we are not very far away from the day where we authenticate via voice bios and retinas. Between now and then we can utilize ownership factor authentication; in plain speak, there is readily available and affordable technology that can seamlessly verify that your customers are who they say they are without interrogation. Smart organizations including banks, are already using technology to perform ownership authentication of caller IDs to make sure the caller is who he said he is without any interrogations whatsoever. You should look for ways to move beyond knowledge based authentications because:

1. It will actually make customers safer. The fraud prevention outcomes of these authentications are better than verifying things like the last four digits of a SSN.

2. It will save you a lot of money. Calculate how much in hard dollars you spend needlessly interrogating customers and you will find a pot of gold big enough to finance your next CX initiative.

3. It will create a superior customer experience.

I, for one, am tired of remembering my childhood pet's name. I called in to change my address – not to be bummed out by the memory of losing my childhood pet.

Smart Data is Here to Save Us

How do you utilize your knowledge about the customer to provide a better customer experience at the interaction level? You do not need any new pieces of data or technology to get started. Take your IVR for example. One of the reasons your IVR is so bad is that you have a one size fits all approach.

I have had many occasions to call AT&T, and every single time it was painful. It was painful because of the gatekeeper from hell - their IVR was an awful gatekeeper. I have covered some tips on improving IVRs on other pages, but the most egregious part of this IVR was that they have more data on their customers than most and can improve the experience greatly by utilizing the data.

When I call in, it verifies the number I'm calling from, asking me if it's the number on my account, I answer in the affirmative. It then asks me why I might be calling and I say, "customer service". It then insists I need to be more specific, providing me a list of options to choose from. I oblige only to be asked what service I have with them (I only had one service with them). This long tree went on to my chagrin. Even if they have no interest in improving the customer experience, they are clearly interested in deflecting calls. They could use data to be better at that and it comes with the byproduct of automatically creating a better customer service experience.

Suppose the IVR was designed so that it identified my phone number, then pulled up my account. It now knows what kind of service I have and the options are narrowed. You could stop here, and already we have progress by eliminating a lot of customer pain. It gets really fun when you take it a step further, given that they have all this data about me, they can safely even predict why I'm calling. If you combine pieces of data strategically, it is shocking just how clairvoyant you can be.

To illustrate what I mean, I remember setting out years ago to accurately predict why our online retail consumers would be calling us and targeted 65 percent. We ended up exceeding that goal. We were very complex internally but once we took an outside-in view, we realized that our consumers saw their reasons for calling in simple terms. So once we mirrored their thinking, our eyes opened and ideas started pouring in. So we started by breaking all inquiries down into two overly simplistic blocks. Then by utilizing more data points, we could get more specific. For example, if we knew the customer's order status, time of day, and expected delivery date, we can predict with higher degrees of certainty why the customer might be calling.

This is real progress, but there is another step you can take fairly easily. You can send all of this rich information in a simple format using CTI (computer telephony integration) technology that's been available for over 15 years, so that you can pass on the data collected to the rep so they know what options have been eliminated and what is still in play.

Then you coach the rep about maximizing the data that the conversation with your customer has provided to continue improving the interaction. A consumer call goes something like this, "Hello Amas, it looks like you are having some trouble with the delivery of your gift. I already found out what the issue is you should be receiving the delivery in the next hour. I have raised the issue with the supply chain and will follow up with my teammates there in the next couple of days". This is an experience that shifts the hard work from your customers and reps to data driven technology that seamlessly gathers all of the necessary data, and enables a contextual, frictionless conversation with your customers.

Continuous and Contextual > Omni-channel

There has been a lot of talk about Omni-channel over the last five years. Omni-channel is the idea of having one continuous conversation with your customer, regardless of channel. Almost all of the focus on this has been on the sales process in practice, attempting to give customers a unified experience regardless of touch point. Retailers are further along on this journey, though I have not seen a use case that shows complete mastery. However, I can order shoes for my son at Famous Footwear online, return it at a store, or order shoes in a store and exchange them for a different color online and have the replacement delivered to my home, and drop off the original pair at the store – you get the idea. Now, when it comes to the other parts of the customer journey, we haven't made as much progress. In fact, I can't have a continuous conversation when I use the same channel twice within an hour.

To me the aspirational goal is to allow for customers to have continuous conversations with you regardless of channel, especially when that conversation is about service. We spent some time earlier discussing how to arrange your channels based on customer issue. There is an opportunity to connect those channels in a way that allows those conversations to not only be continuous, but contextual. Let me point out at this junction that the goal is not to solve the entire problem, but to ensure that all of the critical points of pain are resolved.

With one of my clients, their customers would often email, and then picked up the phone 20 minutes later only to start the same conversation again. The impact of this process was frustrating to the customers and to phone reps who had no insight on the email conversations. Customers often jettison one channel when they realize the service level is unacceptable. They may begin online, noticing that the company has a web form only to submit one and get a response that boasts of "Twenty four hour" response times. Your customer wanting a much faster response from you decides to pick up the phone, only to find that they have to start at the beginning of the process as though they never filled out the web form. You should definitely create a plan to reduce this type of channel hopping.

You can reduce friction further, by smoothing out the transition from channel to channel and there are a number of ways to accomplish this. One method that I especially like is to integrate at least two of your most popular channels. It works this way, assume your two channels are email and phone. You can integrate the two channels so that when a call comes in it does a check of existing emails in the system that hasn't been resolved. If there's a match, you present the rep with that information. So that the call starts with, "Amas, I see you sent an email two hours ago, let me update you ...."

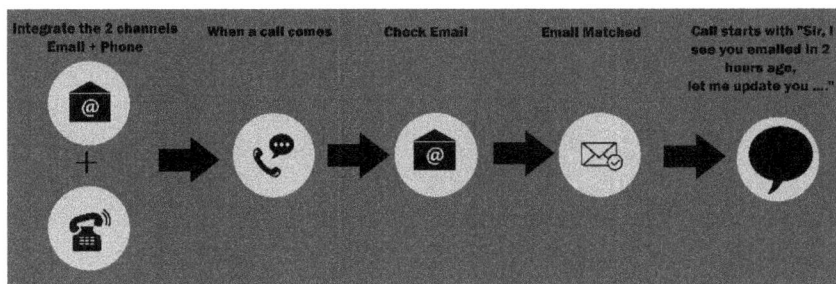

You could actually take this a step further than just providing the information to the next rep, as you could approach the issue a little differently with the context that the customer already tried a different channel. You could choose to prioritize calls that come in for customers that already have an email in queue.

Camera Phones are Evil

"The camera phone is the worst invention of the last decade." – I made that claim a lot when I worked for Teleflora. My reasoning was that for all of the agonizing over the words that can be posted to social media sites, if you were an online retailer that utilizes thousands of independent retail flower shops, nothing was scarier than the camera phone.

In most online retail organizations you have control over the entire supply chain, but in a business where you rely on thousands of third parties to handle the last mile of the fulfillment process, your job can get exponentially harder to execute. Suppose Mr. Smith, a married man, is staying out late and thus decides to send his wife flowers. He goes online to find a very specific yellow bouquet he thinks will convey just the perfect amount of "I'm sorry". The order leaves the website and is then routed to a local florist who is best suited to make this delivery. The florist gets the order and decides for whatever reason to swap out the daisies the bouquet calls for and replace them with chrysanthemums. His lovely wife gets the bouquet and she thinks it is simply gorgeous and she is happy, so all is well right? Wrong! She is so ecstatic that she brings out the evil camera phone takes a picture and then posts it on Facebook to tell the whole world. Everyone is delighted that she got flowers and thus attracts a lot of positive comments on the picture, so all is well, correct? Sure, everyone is happy, except the man who paid for the flowers (the customer). Staring at the picture of the arrangement on Facebook, he notices that although they look great, they aren't the flowers he ordered. Now we have a problem. This was a problem before social media technology or camera phones, and while these occurrences are not prevalent, every one of them was potentially painful.

This problem preceded me and I largely adopted the same practices of everyone else before me, which was to educate the florists. We educated the florists further via more and more channels, making recipes more visible, and gave incentives or penalties to florists for their compliance, or lack thereof. This had limited success. We needed to change florist behaviors and fast, and so I hit the road. I evangelized this message across North America. I explained to florists about the ever-changing consumer. For many years consumers went to florists, gave them a budget and occasion, then the florists made all the creative choices. Now the consumer makes very specific choices online and expects those choices to be honored.

I visited a florist in Texas who had been deviating from the plan on multiple orders and was honest and forthcoming, making it clear to my team that she intentionally deviated from the recipes. She told me that she felt the need to improve upon the designs on the website. Of course I was flabbergasted, but composed myself enough to tell her that when one orders a black pair of shoes online, a nicer pair of brown ones won't do the trick.

As we continued to tackle this problem, I turned to crowdsourcing for help. The idea was that we needed more feedback to help solve this problem. We then created a system that encouraged customers to share their photos with us and then we shared that data (photo and feedback) with the responsible florists to change their behaviors. In other words, let florists hear feedback directly from consumers that are pretty set on getting exactly what they ordered online with pictures to further make the point. Capitalizing on the ability to gather vaster amounts of data like this could improve the customer experience, if you get a little creative on how to use it.

Match-making in Contact Centers

Personalization is a human need. Depending on your company size, you might be providing this by having one rep to x amount of customers, but as your customers' needs grow, technology can help fill the void when that one rep has suddenly more and more customers to satisfy.

My goal here is to help you get focused on the possibilities, especially on the most popular channel, which is *voice*. You want to begin personalizing as soon as the call comes in – start by welcoming them by name. From there the possibilities for personalization are endless, particularly if it is an existing customer. For your existing customers, you have all the data you need to provide a very personalized opening and overall experience.

Your goal should not be to stop at welcoming them by name but to predict with extreme accuracy, why they may be reaching out to you. If you sit around the table with your team, it won't seem so daunting a task once you begin to see patterns in the data. Your goal is not to accurately predict 100 percent of the time, but to chip away at it by tinkering with data combinations. If you think about it, you are already doing some of this in a crude way. Most companies today give you a menu of options based on why you may be calling. Unfortunately, this method is the opposite of personal, as it is usually a one size fits all approach.

Service companies get very clairvoyant when they experience network wide outages, as they know that I am calling because my power is out, and thus put a bland generic message in place to greet all customers to drive abandoned calls and to divert calls. This prediction can be used on an everyday basis. What about prospective customers or even customers without matching info in your databases? You should still attempt to personalize these calls for a couple of reasons. One reason is that it will enhance your customer experience, the second impact is that it will save you valuable time in manually gathering information. The barrier of entry is increasingly lower and lower. In fact, for around three to ten cents per call, you can answer a majority of your calls by first name, even for customers who aren't in your database. You can further personalize the experience after they get to the agent by utilizing all of the rich data that you have collected and passing it on to the rep to provide an even better experience. We have covered predicting why customers may be calling so you can anticipate their needs, but what about customer preferences? How do they like to interact? What is their preference for speed over courtesy? What personality preferences do they have?

The thing about preferences, is that customers share them with you time after time but you chose not to listen. Your customers explicitly and implicitly share these preferences with you every time they interact with you. E-commerce sites are great at utilizing this data during the sales process and even brick and mortar shops are good at this. I frequent a soup and sandwich shop called Cinnamon Deli in Wichita, Kansas. When I walk in, the ladies who work there give me an experience that feels completely personalized based on things I have shared explicitly along with their inferences based on my actions.

I have had many opportunities to utilize data driven technology to personalize service experiences over the years. One of my favorites happened a few years ago when a technology company approached me with a technology that matched reps with the right customers - I was a skeptic. Their value proposition was simple, as they will match the right customer with the right rep and it will result in a better measurable outcome. The thinking is that certain individuals get along better with certain individuals, and there are reasons why different personalities get along better with others. I will leave this theory to the behavioral science experts.. What I can tell you is that it works; you get better sales output and more favorable customer satisfaction results.

In retrospect, I'm not sure why I didn't immediately see the power of this. How many times have you listened to a conversation between two people, let's call them John and Mary, and said to yourself, *"these two are oil and water"*. Mary wants to explain everything and John wants just the facts. She is deliberate and he is always in haste. Somehow they make it through the conversation, but it is painful for all involved. Conversely you can see two complete strangers converse like lifelong friends so effortlessly. What you want is more of the latter and less of the former. Herein lies the power of using data driven technology to match the right customer with the right agent.

How you make this happen isn't overly complicated as the ingredients are the data on your customer and the data on your reps, combined with the needed technology. Let's start with your reps – you already have copious amounts of data on them, so a great place to get started is to transparently invite your reps from the start. You ask them to self-report their personality based on a questionnaire – don't worry about error rate here as the program will self-correct based on customer outcomes.

As for your customers, particularly existing customers, you can draw a line based on the outcomes you have already recorded. You know what customers have had great outcomes with certain personas, so you want to involve your reps pretty early on in the process. It works like this, whenever Mr. Smith calls in and chats with persona type "2" he buys more and gives you a higher CSAT score. If you do not have data on your customers, they are publicly available. There are vendors that will give you customer personas, you simply provide the customers phone number and it returns a value. Skill based routing has been around for some time but this puts that process on steroids. You set this up so that you are able to match customers with the very best reps, based not just on skills but intangibles. You want to always do this with A-B testing so that a percentage of your calls are not routed using this method, so you can constantly measure its efficiency and fine-tune the system.

Data-driven Sales

Call any national brand with awful wait times and select their sales option. In other words raise your hand and tell them you would like to be separated from your wallet, and notice how much shorter your wait is. Don't get me wrong, there is a practical side to doing this as every organization I have been a part of prioritizes sales contacts.

Does it have to end at shamelessly de-prioritizing interactions of paying customers in favor of those who you hope will join the ranks of customers (who will have the honor of being de-prioritized one day)? There are still plenty of other opportunities to optimize the overall sales experience by utilizing data driven technology. It has a bonus side effect of increasing sales and decreasing the cost of acquisitions.

Most of the first impressions your customer experiences with your company happens during the sales process. When I think of the sales process and the customer experience, I would argue that this has been one area where our industry has been creative in the deployment of technology. Millions of dollars have been spent on using data to help anticipate what consumers might buy next.

The area most often overlooked is buyer motivations – the rational and irrational motivation for buying. Most sales processes are set up with a flawed underlying assumption that a customer's motivations for making a purchase are entirely reason and logic based. When I worked in the flower business we sold a lot of flowers to people who didn't like flowers at all – otherwise known as men. If you are a man reading this, then you know exactly what I am talking about. Yes, you buy flowers, but there is not an altruistic motive in your purchase of them.

Men generally buy flowers because of what is in it for them and not because of their affinity for the product. Understanding nuances like this can make a world of difference. Too often we spend too much time trying to connect with customers based on logical reasons to buy, often emphasizing the value of the product

71

itself. While that approach has some legs, it is often when you tap into the emotional reasons for purchasing that you begin to see a higher return.

We hired a consultant who worked with a retail florist to visit us for a day as I was curious on how he increased average order size for his clients. It turns out that his process was beautiful in its simplicity. He simply tells his clients to ask for higher price points. As I studied his process closer and asked questions, I found the secret in his sauce; it was how he asked for the higher price point. It came to a small change on sales flow, *"we flipped things by discussing and taking the card message before asking for any other piece of information"*. It was brilliant insight that is now seen at work in other verticals.

So think about the typical sales process over the phone; it starts with information gathering and prequalifications of sorts. Then later in the conversation, the customer's emotional motivations are explored. The change we made was to start the calls with the emotional and then pivot back to the data gathering. In this case we sold flowers and while they wanted to give us their addresses and names, more than anything they wanted to talk about the most important people in their lives. After all, the reason they are buying flowers is typically for a loved one or a friend, and starting the conversation with the card message not only allowed the call to start with a connection, but also provided valuable intelligence that can increase sales value. For example, you might learn that this gift is from an entire office of fifteen people, changing your positioning of the offer now that it is understood that it is a group gift.

As you can see, the benefits aren't limited to less customer friction but an increase in revenues. Take a case of a client that is in the vacation business; we did a journey mapping session to see the highs and lows of their customer journey to sale. Their reps were focused on helping sellers buy these packages and were having success, but their systems were built to move from screen to screen. They collected customer information and culminated in separating the customer from their credit card number. From the journey map, we learned that the lowest moment on the journey to purchase occurs as they are gathering customer information and the highest point was while discussing the vacation itself. Ideally you want to reduce as many of the low points as you can. So we changed things to maximize the opportunity for emotional connections.

Customer Feedback

It is routine now to solicit feedback. I recently spent most of my day in an airport because my friends at Delta Airlines thought I needed a three-hour delay to enjoy some airport sushi. I was later presented with a survey, they wanted my feedback! It started by acknowledging my delay, then proceeded to ask me, "Mrs. Lincoln, other than that how did you enjoy the play?" Seemingly, after every interaction every company wants feedback. Last week at the Las Vegas airport, the Pei Wei had a slick touchscreen station dedicated to getting my feedback. Clearly the commitment to collecting this feedback is unmistakable and I'm of course told that feedback is needed so they can *improve* the customer experience. Most organizations have a real desire to gauge customer pulse, in fact this need for customer feedback dates back quite some time. Suggestion boxes and comment cards have been in customer facing organizations for many, many years.

The general thought is to listen to customers in the most effective and efficient way possible, and we have come a long way from the days of suggestion boxes. Are company representatives better at meeting customer expectations because of these surveys? What improvements to the customer experience are happening because of the feedback? I rarely fill out transactional surveys from companies. Sure, I look through all the questions for my own research, but most of time I can't bring myself to hit submit. I may be overthinking it, but I worry that my survey data will end up on a server in Utah and that anything I say (or type) will be used against the nice representative sitting in Omaha. I know that data will end up on a scorecard somewhere and judgments will be made, but the representative wouldn't improve and neither will my customer experience.

If we are going to continue to ask for customer feedback, we have an obligation to close the loop with the customers, and particularly when we ask for feedback on employees we should also utilize that feedback for their benefit. Here are a couple of ways to get started.

First, and probably table stakes is following up with every customer who requests follow up; but to be very committed. It is imperative that you begin by letting the general customer base know what improvements you have made specifically as a result of their feedback. Ironically, Delta surprised me positively in this regard. They did a good job recently by sharing the changes they are making as a result of feedback from customers like me.

Secondly, while most companies are good at sharing employee feedback with their employees, it loses its efficacy because most of it isn't actionable, or it is muddled with data about the overall company's inadequacies. They use the scores to reward and punish their employees, and as a barometer on how things are going. I think a different approach would be to explicitly invite the customers to help the agent improve. Tamers is one organization that enables this kind of two-way conversation, that is focused on improving the customer experience by changing the behavior of the employees that are responsible for service delivery.

Collecting feedback is the start of the journey, followed by aggregating the data and following up with the most vocal customers. The real action is in improving customer experience by using the feedback you have to develop your employees. The last and final step is closing the loop with your customer; you can even use this step to brag about how hard you are working to improve the customer experience.

Quantitative systems have been developed to better make sense of all the feedback. I'll focus on a handful of them starting with the net promoter system. I have seen the net promoter system at work first hand. The folks at Bain created and popularized this some years back. It simply asks your customers how likely they are to recommend a Company X to a friend of a colleague. on a scale of 0-10, the 9-10s are promoters, the 0-6 are detractors. You subtract the percent of detractors from the percent of promoters and you have your score.

From first-hand experience, I can tell you there is a strong correlation between this score and customer loyalty – as defined by higher spends per transaction and repeat business. The problem is, it can be a difficult number to move, particularly because it forces the customer to evaluate the totality of the company to make this judgment. Even when you measure NPS at a transactional level, it is still not granular enough to drive change. This leads me to customer effort score (CES). It does a better job of helping you drive change at the transactional level and even when you also measure NPS. The CES can also be a leading measure for NPS. If you are unfamiliar with CES, it asks customers how much effort they had to personally exert to get their issue resolved on a seven-point scale. Unlike NPS, it is focused solely on individual transactions. This is the appeal and the power of CES, as you can begin to drive effort out of transactions which will drive up NPS and loyalty.

None of these programs or scoring systems are perfect, in fact they all have flaws but they generally work if you embrace the principles and don't get too hung up on the methodology.

I was at an industry event a couple years back when the folks at Foresee® introduced a new scoring system called Word of Mouth Index (WOMI). This system introduces a new question, asking customers how likely they are to un-recommend x product or x service etc. It then subtracts the likely to recommend top two boxes from the likely to un-recommend top two boxes. They have a lot of data on how this improves upon the NPS system, and my sense is we are not done and there will be new systems and scores to come. It seems to me that a company like American Express for example, will score well on NPS, CES, and WOMI. The foundational principles are universal regardless of system.

Looking ahead, my instincts tell me that the scale of the scoring system is ready for a change. It seems to me that the eleven point and seven point scales may be going to the way of three point scales. Personally, I think it will result in clearer feedback from customers. I can also tell from personal experiences that there isn't much of a difference between a six and seven in actual customer behavior but in a rigid system like the NPS a "six" is a detractor and a "seven" is viewed as a neutral - which are two different worlds.

Aside from surveys, another area for collecting customer voice is via a focus group. It is a very powerful tool in the toolbox for marketing research or consumer insights, which is also a much-underutilized tool in improving the service experience. Think about all the initiatives that could have used focus groups. Many organizations, particularly B2B organizations use focus groups. A popular version of this is to create advisory committees that include customers to help steer future initiatives. They are often a source for good and are used to help weigh in on future products or services or to participate in testing new products. There are many more ways in utilizing existing customers than the ones mentioned earlier. You could discover more ways by figuring out which area of the customer service process is the biggest pain for your customer when they call in.

I was designing an IVR application for a number of our customers who had extremely low tolerances for *telephony pain*. They were florists who were generally laggards when it came to technology, and to put it mildly, there were hundreds of them who hung on to their Windows 95 and 98 operating systems well into the 2000s. So it goes without saying, that simplicity and ease of use trumped almost anything else. I thought I captured this need well enough in the design, but given the investment, I needed better feedback and intricate data than an email survey could possibly provide.

So we set up a lab of sorts where we could simulate the conditions in their stores. They were complete with computers and phones configured to provide a setting not unlike their stores. To top it off, we included a video camera to capture everything. We then began the simulation, testing out the many use cases for the application. What I was truly interested in was the non-verbal feedback – the horror in their eyes when they heard the hold music. I spent days watching tapes and recording their pain and pleasures in the IVR we built. It pointed out flaws in our system that a survey couldn't have captured.

An often-overlooked source of customer voice is in your own call recordings. I remember 15 years ago when I was summoned by my manager to listen to my call from three weeks earlier. After listening, I couldn't recall the interaction. I noticed after listening to this recording that my manager had a form with grades on it, with pass/fail boxes etc. all adding up to a final score that said I did a good job on that particular call.

The key here is that I did a good job based on my manager's interpretation of the customer's experience and my adherence to internal policies. This process is widely known as quality assurance (QA), for which purports to check for compliance with policy and to ensure a good customer experience. It is on the latter charge of QA that I quibble with the most. You see, coaching employees on what a customer might have felt on a call that happened a couple weeks ago has seen its day in the sun. We no longer need third parties to interpret what the customer experience was on any given customer interaction, as these days, we can ask the customer directly and we can also have the customers help coach the employees.

The way QA is organized, involves managers and QA analysts listening to small samples of calls, scoring the calls, and then drawing conclusions about compliance and customer experience. Those scores often become a big part of the representative scorecards and thus a lot of effort is put in making it *objective,* or more black and white to put it more accurately. In the quest to accomplish this you will find yourself listening to mediocre calls that get a good grade because technically speaking the rep was polite and checked all the boxes. This system always seemed ripe for transformation, though it was odd that we would be guessing how the customer experience was when we could ask the customer directly. Secondly, it didn't sit well with me that we couldn't listen to all of the customer interactions.

The solutions we needed came in the form of a chance meeting with a couple of guys named Scott and Michael at a trade show over five years ago. They tried to sell me on their customer feedback system, so naturally I wanted to know their value proposition. Scott simply said that they would recruit your customers to make your reps better. That began my foray into rethinking how I coached representatives to deliver the great customer experiences they wanted. This system was set up very strategically. After every interaction, the customer is sent an email on behalf of the representative they interacted with, which explicitly asks the customer to help the representative improve their skills by providing them with valuable feedback. This feedback from your customers is used to develop the skills that your representatives need.

Suppose your frontline manager feels like one of your reps is unnecessarily loquacious, and not only is that behavior not building rapport, it is damaging to the experience. To tackle this issue, you could intentionally target customers who interact with that specific rep with a very specific question on that topic, and before you know it, you start getting very useful feedback delivered without the manager's bias. That begins to change or encourage certain behaviors. When I implemented this at Teleflora, the most shocking part was the fact that customers would frequently write longer feedback notes to reps than many of their *end of year reviews*. Looking ahead, I predict that the next step is to include the actual recording of the call or the copy of the written correspondence so the customer can give even better feedback.

The power of customer feedback really is the data inherent in all of those interactions, but they get lost in the manual process involved in sampling interactions. Imagine you take about 500 calls a day and you sample 50 a day for QA. While that may feel like a sufficient sample size, what would it look like if you could listen to every call and eliminate the biases that came from having humans pick calls to listen to? The desire to listen to every call and read every interaction would be solved in the form of voice and text analytics.

Speech Analytics

The first generation of speech analytics was dizzying and widely ineffective but like most technological advancements, it got better with age. I went through one of the early deployments of speech analytics, and needless to say, it didn't go well. With that first stint, we were not very focused. We spent a lot of money on this technology, and wanted to wring as much out of it as possible. It felt like we had overpaid for an all you can eat buffet, and felt the need to over fill our plate with as much as possible to justify the expense. We ended up with more data than anyone knew what to do with, and were largely paralyzed by it all. When I had my second shot, I took a different approach and wanted a much more focused proof of concept that had one outcome in mind, to prove out the technology.

We decided to use speech analytics to improve upsells and cross sells, reviewing every single call. We then wrote queries that could identify calls with an upsell or cross sell opportunity, and whether the representative made the offer attempt. By using this approach, we had 100 percent of the areas of opportunity covered and could laser focus on improving those calls. Once we realized some success, we created another use case, to help identify and root out dead air, and then to identify website issues and so on. What we were able to do is introduce analytics to coaching and save human resources as well. We were able to listen to more meaningful call samples with fewer resources by not aimlessly listening to recordings, but by listening to target sections within the recordings. This made sense for that week's goals. This will arm you with more useful data for your coaching sessions, and you can begin to construct the known elements of successful up sell/cross sells. You can perhaps realize that they are usually best early on in your interaction when the customer is most upbeat. This is information you can now tease out within the rep population.

False Choices

The choice between profits and great customer experience is a false one. Not only can they coexist, but great customer experiences are what generate profits. Your organizations exists to enhance the lives of your customers and as a byproduct of that, you increase your profits and experience growth. If you need more proof, look at some industry research that people like Bruce Temkin and ACSI are doing on this topic. This is not about breaking the bank, as delivering a great customer experiences and being efficient are not mutually exclusive. Au contraire, they are complementary. Particularly if you make sure that the key interactions are intentionally curated. In other words, focus on the ingredients -- liberating structures, empowered people, and data driven technology. Think about them individually and collectively. The customer's needs are only getting more complicated but fortunately, the know-how is more than keeping pace to meet those needs. Customer expectations are rising, and the rate at which they are rising is also increasing. Following the crowd will not deliver experiences customers want. Personalization does not happen by taking permanent residence in groupthinkville. It is by understanding who your customers are, what they want, and then by creating an intentional path to deliver on their expectations. I live and breathe CX. Customer experience is not a strategy, it is the very reason your organization exists.

Let me know how you are doing on your journey, email or text me…I am rooting for you.

You can reach me at amas@amastenumah.com

Amas Tenumah

Bibliography & Notes

INTRODUCTION

BOA & Netflix: http://www.marketplace.org/topics/business/how-consumer-revolt-works

Biased Google Search: http://www.businessinsider.com/evidence-that-google-search-results-are-biased-2014-10

United Airlines Breaks Guitar: https://www.youtube.com/watch?v=5YGc4zOqozo

PART ONE: LIBERATING STRUCTURES

Trust Fall Fail https://www.youtube.com/watch?v=wPOgvzVOQig

Journey Map: You can make journey maps complicated but I think the low-tech maps are just as effective. Here is a sample of one I did with a client recently on http://amastenumah.com/the-curated-experience/

What If Customer Care Doesn't Matter: http://www.forbes.com/sites/kenmakovsky/2014/01/23/where-customer-service-doesnt-matter/

How Did We get Here: History of Call Center: http://www.tmcnet.com/cis/features/articles/301771-history-advancement-the-contact-center-the-customer-experience.htm http://www.zendesk.com/blog/the-history-of-customer-support

Outsourcing – Should You or Shouldn't You Analysis on http://amastenumah.com/the-curated-experience/:

If you can't measure it, what can you measure? Visit http://amastenumah.com/the-curated-experience/ for help with deciding what metrics to use.

Service Level:
For service level goal setting, go to the http://amastenumah.com/the-curated-experience/.

Zappos Long Call:
http://www.huffingtonpost.com/2012/12/21/zappos-10-hour-call_n_2345467.html

ACD: Automated Call Distributor is the machine that routes calls. NPS: Net Promoter System: http://www.netpromoter.com/why-net-promoter/know

CES: Customer Effort Score:
https://www.executiveboard.com/blogs/unveiling-the-new-and-improved-customer-effort-score/

PART TWO: EMPOWERED PEOPLE

Easier to Get into Harvard than SWA
http://www.ballpublishing.com/GrowerTalks/ViewArticle.aspx?articleid=21180

Top Notch – Impact of Leaders on Performance
https://www.td.org/Publications/Blogs/ATD-Blog/2013/01/The-Impact-of-Good-Versus-Bad-Leaders-on-a-Company http://www.forbes.com/sites/glennllopis/2014/01/13/8-qualities-that-make-leaders-extraordinarily-memorable/

Employee First Customer Second Book:
http://www.amazon.com/Employees-First-Customers-Second-Conventional/dp/1422139069

Hiring and Attrition Help: http://amastenumah.com/the-curated-experience/

CEB has a lot of good resources for coaching. Their customer effort book is a great read:
https://www.executiveboard.com/blogs/unveiling-the-new-and-improved-customer-effort-score/

PART THREE: DATA DRIVEN TECHNOLOGY

Stop Interrogating Customers – more on
http://amastenumah.com/the-curated-experience

Call Center Attrition
Voice of the Customer – NPS - http://www.netpromoter.com/home

WOM – http://wordofmouthindex.com/womi-scores/

ROI of CX-
http://www.temkingroup.com/research-reports/the-roi-of-customer-experience/

Future of Biometrics in Banking-
http://whatsnext.nuance.com/customer-experience/cnbc-biometric-authentication-banking/

B2B – Business to Business
QA: Quality Assurance in the contact center
Tammers Partners: http://tamerpartners.com

Acknowledgments

It's been a joy for me to put this book together; I couldn't have done it without the love and support of my family. This has required sacrifices from all of you.

To my loves, Ashley, Aly, Laye, and my son, Tosan, thanks for all of your support.

Amas Tenumah

Testimonials

As a master at operationalizing customer experience, Amas shows how to turn service theories into practical applications that deliver positive bottom-line results. - Flavio Martins, HuffPO Most influential Social Customer Service pro & Author of *Win the Customer: 70 Simple Rules for Sensational Service.*

Amas has a deep passion to see service improve across the board—and he has the know-how and experience needed to show leaders the way. Those who listen will be better equipped to make a positive different for their customers, employees, shareholders--and their own careers. - Brad Cleveland Author, speaker, consultant www.bradcleveland.com

Amas reminds us that Providing exceptional customer service and inspiring customer loyalty requires balance and is both an art, and a science. We must actually use the data we collect pertinent to our customer interactions, avoid over complicating the technology that serves our customers, and ultimately ensure that the people caring for our customers are authentic. - Alison Anderson, Coca-Cola Refreshments, Customer Care

Mr. Tenumah empowers his audience to boldly change the way we go about our work. He dares all of us to lead our profession so that the "customer" and the employee will benefit from the change. - Jonnye GriffinM.A., Program Director

Let me know how you are doing on your Customer Experience Journey, I am rooting for you. Please send me your emails at amas@amastenumah.com or Text me at 405 928 8185.

Amas Tenumah

About the Author

Amas Tenumah is a Technologist turned customer experience expert. He has spent over a decade consulting and leading customer experience programs for numerous companies including: Cox Communications, Teleflora, Coca-Cola, and Convergys Corporation. Tenumah brings a unique perspective to the world of customer experience that he shares regularly on his blog at http://amastenumah.com. He also shares his brand of actionable thought leadership on stage as a keynote speaker at many events. He is a proud dad, avid Yankee fan, and competitive soccer player when home in Oklahoma City.